ROOKIE: THE WORLD OF THE NBA

BY DAVID KLEIN

TEMPO BOOKS

GROSSET & DUNLAP, INC.
A National General Company
Publishers
New York

To Willie and Aaron,
My father and my son
I have learned from both.
And to Carole. Just because.

Tempo Books edition 1973

Copyright © 1971 by David Klein
All Rights Reserved

Library of Congress Catalog Card Number: 71-163264
ISBN: 0-448-05565-1
Tempo Books is Registered in the U. S. Patent Office

This edition is published by arrangement with
Cowles Book Company, Inc.
A subsidiary of Henry Regnery Company

Published simultaneously in Canada
Printed in the United States of America

ROOKIE

What is it like for a gifted college player who decides to put all his talents and determination on the line, to achieve superstardom in the harsh, competitive world of the NBA? Night after night, in city after city he must pursue his private dreams in a fishbowl of public existence.

Each of the rookies in this book had an enviable talent, and at the same time his own high hurdle to be cleared—the war with himself and his own shortcomings.

Here is Kareem Abdul-Jabbar, the giant of a man who had to battle against abuse and live up to extraordinary goals; Calvin Murphy, a "shrimp" in the land of giants; and Pete Maravich, who fought not only his competitors but his famous father's reputation. Neal Walk, Geoff Petrie, Bob Lanier, Dave Cowens, Jo Jo White—the legends of all are uncovered in this fascinating account of breaking into NBA big time.

Contents

	Acknowledgments	vii
	Introduction	1
1	Lew Alcindor	9
2	Calvin Murphy	50
3	Pete Maravich	83
4	Five for the Money	117

Acknowledgments

The amount of assistance that I needed in the preparation of this book came as a rather ego-deflating revelation. Bravely gripping my typewriter with both hands and feeling very fortunate to have so many friends, I offer gratitude to Les Woodcock, Bob Roesler, Pete Finney, Phil Pepe, Bob Casey, Nick Curran, Mike Shaw, Richie Guerin, Larry Costello, Jimmy Bukata, and Frank Blauschild. Special thanks go to Ron Buehl, for the chance to write the book. In addition, I would like to thank Carole, Aaron, and Mindy for keeping the noise down to a roar during those many long Sunday afternoons. Finally, not only the players treated in this book but many others, collegians and professionals, were kind enough to answer with patience questions they no doubt have heard hundreds of times before. It was George Bernard Shaw who said that in order to write a single book, one must read a thousand written before on the same subject. I only wish G.B.S. had offered some tips on the proper handling of statistics and newspaper clips.

DAVE KLEIN
July, 1971

Introduction

T HERE are several of them.

They are young men in a hurry, to whom life has become the steady tattoo of the bounce of a basketball, the glare of lights reflected off the glossy floorboards of the country's most elaborate and costly arenas, the rumble and the roar of a cheering crowd, the rigors of a never-ending schedule of games played against the finest practitioners of the sport in the world.

Night after night, in city after city, from October to May, they pursue their private dreams in a fishbowl of public existence.

Some of them were rookies in the 1969–1970 season. Others were rookies a season later. All are different—different sizes, different tasks, different styles—yet they are linked to one another by a common bond, their determination to become stars, to excel in the National Basketball Association.

Each approaches his goal with different tools and varying skills, for each has been gifted with deep and diverse abilities. They are not all of equal potential, but that is not the issue at hand. They are all making it, each in his own way, and their accomplishments serve as the vehicle from which to launch *Rookie: The World of the NBA*.

There are two common denominators in these young men. One is their fascinating and enviable talent. The other is that each has been forced to overcome an obstacle, which in some cases was nothing more adverse than a handicap of circumstances but, nevertheless, a hurdle to be cleared. They each have had to wage war with themselves and their critics.

Lew Alcindor's very greatness was his burden. He brought his special brand of magic to the Milwaukee Bucks as one who had rarely experienced defeat. He had to adjust to the new experience of losing, for no team and no individual can escape the inevitable reality of defeat inherent in the rigorous NBA schedule. The level of competitive quality is too close, even between champion and last-place team, for one club to dominate absolutely.

Alcindor did not have to learn to play the pros' game, for he intimidated them from the day he signed a contract. Rather, he has had to live with the demands of his fans and with the fact that he is different and will always remain so. Indeed, it was difficult for him to accept the truth of his physical dimensions, to know that because he stands three inches taller than seven feet, he can never find a place to hide.

Alcindor, then, is a brooding giant of a man, often moody and frequently churlish. But to understand the uniqueness of his position and the enormity of his talent is to understand his behavior and his desires. Achieving stature in basketball has been easy for Lew Alcindor.

Achieving a rapport with himself and with those around him and accepting what and who he is has been more difficult.

Calvin Murphy's problem is that he is too short. He measures only 5′9″ and everyone knows that anyone 5′9″ is far too short to compete in the NBA, where the guards stand 6′4″ and sacrifice nothing to their size in the way of speed and ball-handling. But Calvin is doing it, and he has become a favorite of fans across the country and a bright promise to the San Diego Rocket supporters.

Murphy's jump shot, flicked away at the height of an impossible leap, slips as easily through the NBA nets as it did when he played for Niagara College in upstate New York, where three times he achieved All-America honors. His cat-like and mercurial speed produces defensive efforts that still result in the stolen dribble, in the deflected pass, and in the steal and subsequent easy lay-up. His ball-handling delights the crowds and befuddles his opponents, whether they are Earl Monroe or Walt Frazier or some obscure college guard.

Calvin rose to the Herculean challenge of daring the pros to prove that he was too small. They have not been able to do so yet, and they probably never will.

Pete Maravich, perhaps even more than Alcindor, has had to live with his dazzling reputation, which followed him from college at Louisiana State University to the Atlanta Hawks, who paid him more than $2 million as their top draft choice of 1970. Maravich cannot pretend to be other than what he is—a showman, an excellent passer, an accurate shooter, and a ball-handler of consummate skill. But his showmanship has alienated many of the pros, and the fact that his father, Press Maravich, was his coach at LSU and tailored the team's offense to build Pete into a high scorer indicated to many that Pete has been badly spoiled. They felt that he would have to learn humility before he could become an integral part of a pro team. With his famous floppy socks and long hair and his good looks, Maravich was the envy of every pro who did not receive equal money and fanfare.

"Pistol Pete" has not yet set the NBA on fire. He has wisely been moved in gradually by his coach, Richie Guerin. He has slowly been given more playing time, thereby accumulating a storehouse of experience. But there have been nights when he has extracted hysterical, almost reverent applause for his dexterous passes, for his long jump shots, and for his powerful charisma.

The seasoned veterans have begun, grudgingly, to admire Pete's talents in public. Such praise for a rookie is rare and consequently precious. No one has doubts any longer that Pete Maravich will soon be a superstar. There are those who say he is that already.

Neal Walk, on the other hand, has had to prove that his collegiate heroics, his All-America career at the University of Florida, was not merely the result of a zealous publicity department. He is not a naturally graceful or imposing athlete, but he was considered the second-best center in the crop of graduating seniors from which the NBA made its 1969 draft selections.

Being second-best did not indicate that he approached the quality of Lew Alcindor. It meant, rather, that after Lew there were few good centers, among whom Neal Walk was the best. Yet he was the second player drafted, picked by the Phoenix Suns after they lost the toss of a coin to Milwaukee. The jubilant Bucks immediately claimed Alcindor, a move that surprised no one. The Phoenix selection was, however, surprising. It had been assumed that the Suns would go for a forward or a guard, deferring their choice of a center until the next draft.

Thrown into this pressure situation, Walk has begun to prove that his value to the Suns was not overestimated, despite the fact that he is neither overpowering nor gifted with unusual skills. Walk's forte is determination and strength, factors that made up for his lack of finesse. These assets are valuable to a man who has much to prove.

In 1970, Bob Lanier was as highly prized as Lew Alcindor had been in 1969. He was the year's top bigman, a 6'11", 275-pound center from St. Bonaventure. Lanier could shoot as well from the outside as Willis Reed of the New York Knicks, and his disruptive muscling under the boards was enough to flatten men bigger than Reed. He had taken his Brown Indians to the brink of an NCAA championship when he suffered a stunning knee injury in the final moments of a game that had long since been decided. But the surgery, performed immediately, repaired the damage to the extent that Lanier was drafted first by the Detroit Pistons, who had first choice in the league.

Lanier never played against Alcindor in collegiate basketball, although he often spoke of his desire to do so. Their first meetings have not lacked excitement, for only Lanier has the necessary ability to match Lew. He has not hit the NBA with the impact that Alcindor registered, but no one will deny his coming greatness.

"Geoff Petrie? He won't do," said the blasé fans who needed only a cursory glance at his college background to make their prediction. Petrie is a Princeton product, and everyone knows that scholars, not athletes, choose Ivy League schools. But the scouts looked in wonder as Petrie, a 6'4" guard, proved there was nothing he could not do on a basketball court. The expansionist Portland Trail Blazers made him their first draft selection and looked on as he was voted to the All-Star team as a rookie as well as sharing the Rookie of the Year award at the conclusion of the season.

Petrie's name hovered up near the top of the league's

scoring column during his rookie season, and now there are no disbelieving fans. They all know that when the Trail Blazers chose the educated and talented athlete, they took a definitive step in building a competitive NBA team.

The Boston Celtics, once the scourge of the league, had fallen on hard times and demeaning seasons when the inevitable retirement announcement came from their famous center, Bill Russell. A few poor years followed, until general manager Red Auerbach picked, on the first round of the 1970 draft, a relatively unheralded Florida State University center named Dave Cowens—"too small," a 6'9", to be a center. But Russell was 6'9", and Auerbach knew what Cowens could do.

He was right. Cowens has revitalized the Celtics. He has become a rebounder of amazing skill, and he has shown he can score. He can play excellent defense. Indeed, he received many votes, early in the season, as Rookie of the Year. Ultimately, he shared the honor with Petrie, the first time the award had been voted to two rookies.

Cowens has a teammate on the Celtics, a second-year guard named Jo Jo White, a hero of the United States' Gold Medal victory in the 1968 Olympics basketball competition. He, too, was a first round choice, and he, too, was thought to be too small. White is 6'2", and he has become one of the NBA's top guards. In the fast-break style of the Celtics, White has become the source of power. He can shoot from a great distance with accuracy, and his defense is a study in tandem movement with his opponent.

Auerbach picked two plums from the pudding of college athletes, and he has his Celtics well on their way back to the pinnacle of professional basketball.

These, then, are the young stars. They each have a story to tell. Developing into a professional is never easy for the rookie involved, but when each has had to master more than the improvement of skills, the successfully completed task serves as a lesson in dedication and an inspiration to other young men who imagine themselves as pro basketball players one day.

There is little doubt that these heroes will remain NBA stars for a long time. How they reached their individual mountaintops bears telling.

1

Lew Alcindor

THERE is an electric attraction and an aura of magnetism surrounding Lew Alcindor.

There is a fascination about him that makes him unique, even in a world of very tall people.

It is not only because, at 7'3", he is so very much taller than the rest of them, taller, in fact, than anyone playing professional basketball today, but also because he is decidedly better than any of them. It is not his status as a superstar, either, although he may be the best of all the superstars produced by the game of basketball. Nor is it his brooding, solemn, puzzling demeanor that enhances the mystery of Lew Alcindor.

It is, rather, the ease with which he dominates and intimidates the opposition, the effortless perfection and the flawless development of his talent. Lew Alcindor is like no one else who has played this game, with the possible exception of Wilt Chamberlain, who was, a decade ago and in a less refined package, what Lew is now.

Long before he finished high school, before the relentless drive to enlist him in college started, Lew had already graduated from the toughest, most demanding basketball school in the country—the parks and playgrounds of New York City. He quickly became a hero in this unique social structure, this world of jump shots and rebounds, this existence marked by the constant bounce of the ball on black-topped asphalt or cracked concrete. Lew Alcindor was a legend by the time he reached his early teens. It simply remained for the rest of the world to discover what the kids on the streets of Harlem knew all along—that this gangly and gentle youth was going to become the best center in the history of basketball.

But if the temptation is to picture Lew as a product of those streets, of the poverty-pocket nowhere called Harlem, it would be a hasty and inaccurate assumption.

Lew was reared by his parents to appreciate the advantages of an education and to think beyond the immediacy of basketball and the companionship found on the streets. The acquisition of an education became his long-range goal. He was sent to Power Memorial High School in Manhattan, a Catholic school run by the Irish Christian Brothers, because of its academic, not athletic, reputation. Of course, the Brothers were pleased that such a basketball celebrity was to become a member of the team as well as the student body, but his parents' choice of the school was based solely on education. It is just as certain, however, that the other Catholic and parochial schools in New York City that offer scholarships were downcast at his decision.

To his father, however, the decision was important only in that a search for the proper educational atmosphere had been completed.

"Basketball," says Ferdinand Lewis Alcindor, Sr., "was a natural discovery for Lewis because of his height and his athletic ability. But if he had been a 'normal' boy, if this game had never become part of his life, we would have tried to lead him in exactly the same direction. No one can make it today without an education, and no one can do himself any good at all by running with the street gangs.

"We were determined to bring Lewis up properly, as best as we could, and to give him respectable goals and guides in life. Of course, we are intensely proud of all his basketball accomplishments and of all the honors he has received, but we are just as proud that he got his education, his college degree. Also, because we know what he went through as a youngster, being so tall and all, we are doubly proud of the way he stood up to all the pressures he had to face, all that staring and pointing at him.

"When it all started, we were afraid of how he would react. But we never had to worry about Lewis. We were honestly surprised at how well he handled himself. We are satisfied now that he is a decent person, sensitive and educated and aware, and we like to think it would have turned out that way regardless of basketball. He had to be a man first, then an athlete. We never pushed him to play ball, but we did push him to do the right things and to make what we felt were the right decisions in his life."

No man ever came to play as ready and as well equipped for star status as did Lew Alcindor. His height worked to his advantage in more than the obvious ways, for when he began to play, it became apparent that he had not sacrificed coordination and quickness for height. He was disjointed and awkward only for a short period of time and far earlier in his adolescence than normal in such instances of rapid growth.

Thus Lew was as agile as a guard and as quick as a

forward while pushing the height of seven feet in high school. He was truly one of the special ones, and it took very little time before the scouts and coaches at major colleges learned of his talent, his potential, and his whereabouts.

They began snapping at his heels while he was a sophomore, bombarding him with glowing descriptions of such-and-such a university and such-and-such a program. It quickly became intolerable, and Alcindor began to lose patience and concentration. Help was needed right away, before he considered turning away from his basic goals.

Enter Jack Donohue.

Jack is a genuinely funny man. He is quick-witted and gregarious, friendly and direct, prized as a speaker at dinners and awards ceremonies. He is now the head basketball coach at Holy Cross, having taken the job shortly after Alcindor graduated from Power Memorial. Donohue was the coach at Power, but he was also much more. He was advisor and friend, protector and counselor. To Lew Alcindor, this was no doubt the more important facet of what Donohue stood for.

Donohue is ruddy-faced and gray-haired, and his eyes take on a pleasant twinkle just before he is going to deliver a punch line. He is bubbly and witty, eager to talk and anxious to extract a chuckle from his audience.

When Holy Cross was scheduled to play the University of California at Los Angeles in New York's Madison Square Garden, in a season when Alcindor was a Bruin sophomore and was already rewriting record books and defensive strategies, Donohue was asked how he planned to prepare for the onslaught of this familiar giant.

"I've been thinking about that," he began, and the twinkle in his eyes was there from the start. "First, I am going to call him and remind him of all the good times we had together. Then I am going to ask him to remember all the nice things I did for him. Then I am going to work on his sympathy. I'll tell him I'm sick and couldn't take a defeat. Then I'll either cry a lot or cut my throat."

Donohue recalls their first few meetings with a smile, savoring the memory of his initial encounters with this outstanding athlete. He was Lew's closest friend throughout those hectic high school days, and he did an exceptional job of shielding him from those who relentlessly sought him out. Jack protected Lew from the constantly increasing number of newspaper reporters, magazine editors, and photographers who attempted to build him into a celebrity before he was able to handle it.

"When I first saw him," Donohue remembers, "he was playing for the St. Jude's Grammar School team in New York. I thought I had reached the point all basketball coaches hit one day if they care about their jobs. You know, I had been dreaming of the perfect big kid for so long that I thought I had started hallucinating. But there he was. A little gangly, maybe. And awkward. But he really had the tools, and he had no idea of the tremendous talent he possessed. He was so far superior to the usual tall kid I somehow felt he wasn't real. It was a coach's dream, but other coaches wake up. I was wide awake and there he was. It was unnerving.

"He was kind of quiet, you know, kind of moody. He was very self-conscious about his height, and he wasn't sure how to react to people. You know, I guess it's natural for people to stare at somebody that tall, and to ask the silly questions, like 'How's the weather up there?' The older players can do it. They realize they are tall and they accept it as a fact of life. But Lew was just a kid, and it confused him. I think there were times when he wished he wasn't so tall, when he wished he was like the rest of the kids. He was searching for an identity, and I know it was a terribly difficult part of his life."

The acceptance of his physical state arrived gradually, and with it Lew began to revel in the delights of his talent, in his achievements on the court. He came to love the game, both the playing of it and the lure of it.

Working diligently under Donohue's tutelage, Lew began to perfect the gifts he had been granted. "He never minded hard work," Jack adds, "he could run all day and he never objected to long practice. When he did something wrong, I told him what it would take to correct it, and he decided that as long as he was going to be a basketball player, the worst thing that could happen to him was to be laughed at. There is nothing sadder than a bad big man. So he worked and worked harder, and it didn't take long for improvement to show."

It was Donohue who prodded him to perfect the ominous hook shot, which only Alcindor seems capable of shooting at the basket from a downward angle. He learned the fadeaway jump shot that has proved virtually impossible to block. He absorbed the theories of rebounding, of using his body as well as his height to secure position, of not reaching for the ball but jumping for it, of not tapping it around and not slapping at it but grabbing it firmly with both hands. He learned defense, which for him has become a rare art form. He mastered the necessary timing to block shots without committing fouls.

He learned to dominate, and he soon became a psychological asset for his high school. He aided his team by simply walking out to the center circle to start the game. Gradually, as the complete Alcindor began to emerge, he flashed the signs of what he would become, of what he would be capable of doing as a professional, and the prospect was staggering. Jack Donohue had brought this youth to the brink of greatness at an age when most young athletes, even the special ones, are only starting to grasp the fundamental skills.

In his varsity seasons at Power Memorial, Lew Alcindor experienced defeat only once, a loss that snapped a national record seventy-one consecutive wins. His varsity record hit 79–1 when he graduated. That defeat, in a second meeting arranged with DeMatha High School of Washington, D.C., which has produced many top college and pro stars, was witnessed by fourteen thousand people in the University of Maryland fieldhouse. Power Memorial never lost a New York City League game, and won three consecutive city high school championships.

"When we lost that game," Donohue remembers, "Lew cried. He blamed himself for the defeat [he had scored only sixteen points], and he felt absolutely miserable. I tried to tell him that there would have been no way for us to have seventy-one in a row without him, that it was far from being his fault, that we had just run into possibly the second-best high school team in the country. I said DeMatha might have beaten us by thirty points without him on our side [the score was 46–43, DeMatha electing to slow down the game after it took an early lead]. But it didn't help. I never saw a kid who hated to lose as much as Lew. You know, I really think we had forgotten how to lose.

"It's difficult to admit," Donohue continues, "but I felt we never were in danger of losing a single game when Lew was with us. I knew that somehow he would do enough for us to win. We built a confidence in him that swept up the rest of the team, and they all played better because he was there. I'm not sure if I can explain that, but I'll try.

"Take a kid, for instance, who has a pretty good jump shot, say from twenty feet. If he starts off a game and misses his first five or six shots, the tendency would be for him to lose his confidence. He'll begin to hesitate before shooting many more times. I guess the fear of being embarrassed figures in there somewhere, but it should be more of a reluctance to hurt the team's chances. Nobody likes to see a gunner who is missing but never stops taking the shots.

"But by playing with Lew, that problem never came up. I mean, if a kid was cold, Lew would just keep on getting the rebounds, and then he'd either score from underneath or pass the ball out again. His presence under the boards was a great source of confidence to the rest of the team. Also, you must figure the reality of what he could do. I mean, if a kid plays for a team and the star has just scored forty-five points and pulled in thirty rebounds, the feeling of invincibility gets to be contagious. The other four starters were loose and relaxed. They played to their fullest potential because Lew was so automatic and so harmful to the other team. There really wasn't any pressure on the rest of them, so they could afford the luxury of playing relaxed. As you know, that's the ideal mental attitude to take into a game.

"But you must admit it is kind of hard to get that attitude without having the super player to make it happen. Just watching him do his thing was usually enough for the other kids to get hopped up. They'd see him take down a rebound and go right back up with it for a stuff, or they'd watch him block a shot and catch the ball in midair, and they'd begin to feel they couldn't do anything wrong either. Or, if they did, Lew would be there to bail them out. It was a great atmosphere to coach in because they were so thoroughly enjoying themselves they were able to take all the coaching I could dish out, and they were able to learn faster.

"I felt sorry for the other teams," Donohue continues, "I really did. But was I going to tell him not to score too much? Not to block so many shots? I couldn't put him on the bench just to even up the game. Lew was the kind of kid who comes along just once, and I was lucky to be working at the school where he showed up. I can't deny I enjoyed being identified as his coach or that it hasn't helped me since. But it was a great responsibility, too, because I wondered whether I was capable of developing a talent like his. I really wondered. I mean, you just don't expect to find kids like that in high school. Not kids that tall and that good."

Lew Alcindor was born April 16, 1947. His given name is Ferdinand Lewis Alcindor, Jr., but he's not called that—ever.

He was 5'4" in the fourth grade, but his father is 6'2" and his mother 5'11", so his height was not a surprise. But by the time he was ten he stood 6'3", and three years later he had sprouted another five inches, to 6'8". When he was seventeen he had reached the 7' mark.

Now the pros who must play against him, who must find some way of neutralizing his presence, insist that he is still growing. "It's kind of scary," says Willis Reed, the captain of the New York Knicks and, at 6'10", one of the smallest NBA centers, "but each time we play Milwaukee, it seems Lew is a little taller. I know it isn't likely, but you do have to stop and think about it, you know? Right now, Lew is taller than Wilt. I mean, if I'm 6'10", you understand, I can figure for myself just how big Lew is by standing next to him. And then I can stand next to Chamberlain when I get the chance. I swear Lew is 7'3". Maybe more. But when you play somebody that big, you can usually count on them not being real quick or agile. Big, sure, and hard to move, and harder to go around, but not like a cat. Not like a forward. Still, I had some chance in his rookie year, because he didn't know how little he had to do to beat people. I mean, he would make a lot of fakes, try dribbling a lot, dance around out there with the ball, and maybe even try some cute stuff, and all the while he was just wastin' time. It gave me a chance to knock the ball away, or to get into the right position so that he would have a tougher shot when he finally went up with it.

"But when he learns to save motion and effort and just to turn to the basket and shoot, I doubt if anyone in this league will be able to play with him, or even to stay with him. I hope I get a lot of basketball played during the next few years, because I surely don't want any part of that cat when he gets as good as he can be."

No one ever doubted that Lew would be an instant hit as a pro. After all, he had showed the country his potential for three varsity seasons at UCLA. What years they had been: three times All-America; three straight NCAA championships; three times the NCAA tournament's Most Valuable Player. It seemed he could score as many points as he chose and snare as many rebounds as he wanted. They even changed the rules to stop him, banning the dunk shot in time for his junior season, because he was threatening to destroy the game.

Back at Power Memorial, in his senior year, when the scouts and the colleges were clamoring for a decision, Alcindor had been the most sought-after high school player in the country. By then Donohue thought he had seen all the letters, heard all the offers, and listened to all the promises; but it had only started.

"It got absolutely frantic," he remembers. "I had all the letters sent to me, and his parents forwarded unopened any that got through to their house. They kept changing their telephone number, but people continued to find out the new ones. I told Lew not to talk to any scouts, coaches, or members of the press. I kept them all away during practices, and I refused to let them talk to him before or after a game. You just can't believe how persistent these people were. It was never-ending.

"I suppose a lot of people thought I was unfair and out of line, but I was just trying to protect Lew. He was so confused by all the offers, and he didn't know what to say to all those vultures who wanted to get his ear. I decided it would be easier for me to put a blanket over him, to keep him away from all those people. Any decision that was going to be made would be made by himself and his parents. I never tried to influence him, even when I thought I had a pretty good chance to get the Holy Cross job.

"Would I have wanted to take Lew up there with me? Ask me if I want to keep breathing every day—the answer is the same. I mentioned it to him once, and he took a trip to Boston just to make me happy, but he never wanted Holy Cross, and I never pushed it. I kept thinking it would be a conflict of interests situation. I mentioned it once to him, as I said, and he knew I was considering the job. But he was always honest with me and he just said he wasn't interested. It never got very serious."

There were nearly 250 colleges and universities in the Alcindor sweepstakes, all of which had, in one form or another, made presentations to Donohue. He heard all the offers and several thinly disguised inducements directed at him. "I think I was offered about a dozen top jobs," he smiles now, "contingent on bringing Lew with me. I never even answered those people."

It was a monumental decision, and Lew kept pushing it off. Slowly, he and his parents and Jack Donohue narrowed down the final choice to five colleges. "It was, I guess, a final choice of wanting to stay near home or going away," Alcindor says. "I didn't want to go away for the sake of going. I had always been intrigued by California, and I guess I had decided that if I ever left New

York, it would be for there. But I had good reasons for staying close to home, too.

"My parents were there and my friends, and it was my hometown, and I knew it pretty well. I knew I could get to be well-known if I stayed in New York. And I would have had a lot of fun, too, playing ball in the city. There were lots of good schools I could have picked, because I never had any trouble with my grades.

"Finally, I narrowed my choice down. UCLA was one. St. John's and NYU were the two local ones. Michigan was attractive, and Boston College was the other one. I had gone to California to meet coach [John] Wooden, and I found him to be very pleasant. I liked the campus and the weather. I had never been pressured by the coach, which was in his favor. He gave me the impression that he would be very glad to have me, but if I chose some other school, well, fine. I tend to shy away from highly aggressive people. They make me nervous. I did go up to Holy Cross, and I was impressed by their campus. But I did it for coach Donohue. I just didn't want to go there. I guess once he knew he was going to take the job, he felt he had to ask me to see the campus. I understood that, and I went with an open mind. But he made sure to tell me that Holy Cross was hiring him because he was a good coach, not as a man who could deliver Lew Alcindor. So I felt no pressure at all when he asked me to take a look. I respected him for that a great deal."

The five choices were all fine schools, with educational opportunities as wide-ranging and as nationally recognized as their athletic programs. Lew Alcindor was seventeen years old, and he had been heralded from coast to coast with all the fanfare of a superstar. Coaches everywhere knew his name, knew what he could do for them and how badly they wanted him on their teams. No one, of course, knew the names of the five schools he had selected from the unbelievable number of offers, no one except Lew and his parents and his coach. Finally, they decided that a brief public press conference would be the best way to announce his decision.

"That way," Donohue says, "it would be over and done with. Everyone would know. If Lew told just UCLA, he still would have been bothered by the rest. Making it public would solve that problem. I also felt it would give him a chance to get some exposure and some experience in dealing with the press, which I had not allowed before. I knew it was something he would have to learn to handle. All in all, I think it worked out for the best."

The date was May 4, 1965. The setting, appropriately, was the gymnasium at Power Memorial, the scene of some of Alcindor's most famous exploits. Big Lew and his coach stood in the center of the court, surrounded by television lights and cameras and a battery of radio microphones and more than fifty newspapermen. The size of the turnout surprised Donohue, for not nearly that many had been invited. Lew Alcindor was big news in a big city.

Finally, after waiting nervously, shifting his weight from foot to foot, Lew was given the nod by Donohue. He cleared his throat a few times, bent to speak into microphones that already were raised to their fullest height, and said in an even voice:

"This fall, I'll be attending UCLA in Los Angeles. That's the decision I came to. It has everything I want in a school."

There was cheering on the UCLA campus and a great gnashing of teeth everywhere else.

There is a great image of California that abounds across the rest of the United States. It holds that California is more fantasy than fact, more frill than reality. The sun always shines, and the people are all beautiful, and the sky is always blue but flecked with just enough flossy marshmallow clouds to make it look better. No one cries, and no one has problems in California. It is the promised land.

"Baloney," says Lew Alcindor. "California has the same kind of people as you'll find anywhere else. You have nice folks and you have bigots. Men still get up to go to work, and ghetto children here still have as little as the kids in New York's ghettos.

"I guess I was a little disillusioned about California, but that kind of an experience is necessary for a person to grow emotionally. I was homesick, too. I was lonely, and I started wondering if I had done the right thing. Not that I was unhappy at UCLA, you know. The kids were great, the coaches were honorable, and the school was all they said it was. But I was eighteen years old and I was away from home for the first time, and I was a little bit loose. You know what I mean?"

Lew was lost and confused. But that feeling stopped the moment he took the court, the instant he pulled on his sneakers and began shooting and running. Then he became special, and on a court anywhere, Lew Alcindor was at home.

"I remember his first game as a freshman," a Los Angeles sportswriter recalls. "The varsity had won two straight NCAA championships, and most everybody was back for another season. It was a good team, a very good team. At UCLA, the first game of the season, by tradition, is between the freshmen and the varsity. Sort of a warmup, you know, to get the varsity loose and to show the freshmen just how far they had to go.

"But this freshman team was kind of unique. The rest of the kids might have made it a good game without Alcindor. With him, it was a joke. The varsity was the number one team in the country and the number two team on its own campus."

That was November 27, 1965. It was still football season, and the UCLA gridmen were closing in on another superb finish. The pro Rams were in the midst of a chase for an NFL championship. But more than ten thousand showed up at Pauley Pavilion, the school's new fieldhouse, to watch this intrasquad contest. They might have come anyway, for John Wooden, a recruiter with an uncanny success record, had gathered a stellar crop of high school stars. Indeed, four other kids had been acclaimed as High School All-America selections.

There were Lucious Allen, a 6'3" guard from Kansas City, Missouri; Lynn Shackleford, a 6'5" blond-haired beach boy from Burbank; Kenny Heitz, a 6'4" guard from Santa Maria, California; and Kent Taylor, another 6'4" guard from Houston, Texas. And then there was Alcindor, who had inched up past the 7'1" mark and developed his skills to the point of near-perfection.

The freshmen won the game, 75–60. Lew scored thirty-one points, took down fifteen rebounds, and devastated the proud championship varsity. Fred Schaus, the general manager of the Los Angeles Lakers of the NBA, sat in the stands that night and ate his heart out. "I admit I was a little shaken," he recalled. "The kid was just eighteen, and I was unconsciously comparing him to the NBA centers. He had the moves and the shots, and he knew what to do underneath. I found myself saying 'he's playing defense like Bill Russell' and then, a little later, 'he's as strong as Thurmond,' and 'he's as tough to box out as Wilt.' I'll tell you, it was an experience. And he was only a freshman. I started getting excited watching him play, knowing that as good as he looked, he would get twice as good, three times, by the time he finished college."

Sadly, that was the high point of his freshman season.

Not that he did not excel—he did. Not that he did not intimidate and begin to build his legend—he did. He just ran out of competition. No freshman team—or junior college team—was able to offer the type of test he needed. He found himself playing against centers who were 6'3" in a forced crouch to play defense against them, scoring at will with an ease that bordered on the ridiculous.

The only competition he found was during squad workouts, when he could go against the varsity or work one-on-one with Jay Carty, a 6'8" graduate student retained as an "assistant freshman coach" which, in truth, meant an Alcindor coach. Carty worked with him and pushed him, prodded and fouled him intentionally, trying to anger him and motivate him to reach beyond what he could get away with against the 6'3" centers.

The season ended with the freshmen 21–0. Alcindor had averaged 33.1 points and 21.5 rebounds per game. He broke the school's freshman rebounding and scoring records long before the season had finished. The team was too good, and the opponents fell like flies. The average score for the freshmen was 113.2 points per game. The enemy averaged 56.6. In one incredibly mismatched affair, Lew was the chief wrecking agent for a team that turned a game into a rout. The Baby Bruins beat the Citrus Junior College team by 103 points!

Lew grew lethargic from lack of competition. He looked forward to the team scrimmages and the practices and the sessions with Carty while he accepted with boredom yet another scheduled freshman game. What did the Palomar Junior College or the San Diego Community College teams offer Lew Alcindor? *Nothing*.

But Lew was happy as a member of the UCLA student body, even if he did miss New York City. He grew to respect and admire coach Wooden, and he established a close rapport with his teammates, especially Lucious Allen, with whom he shared a room. "If only they could take the school and the campus and transplant it to the middle of New York," he said once, "then things would be just perfect."

But he continued to smile at the erroneous reports that said he would transfer to Michigan or St. John's. "I made my decision," he said, "and I really do like it. I just have to get used to being homesick for a while. But it will stop."

The freshman year was finished, the Mickey Mouse basketball completed, and a varsity career beckoned Lew Alcindor. He had three years in which to prove he was capable of making all those advance notices bear fruit, three years in which to show he was, indeed, the best big-man in the country.

On December 3, 1966, Lew Alcindor became a varsity performer. It was the opening game of the season, a night meeting against Southern California. The place was packed to the limits of the fire laws, with more than thirteen thousand jamming Pauley Pavilion. They had come to see Lew's debut, and he did not disappoint them.

Lew scored fifty-six points, setting an all-time UCLA record in his first varsity appearance. He dominated the backboards, and he was an octopus on defense. The ball seemed to shrink when it entered his hands. He cradled it like an orange, throwing long passes downcourt with a baseball pitcher's motion. He jumped to catch lofted passes, and on his way down he reached out to stuff the "pellet" through the hoop. It was awesome and overpowering, and to coach Wooden it was a bit frightening.

"He does frighten me a bit, at times," said the quiet-spoken, scholarly man, perhaps the finest basketball coach in the college ranks. "He does not yet grasp the full impact of what he can do. But he is coachable and self-sacrificing and a team player. I am completely aware of what his presence on the court does to other teams, and I can feel for them. He is awesome."

Those words had a familiar ring. They were the same sentiments expressed by Jack Donohue when he defined Alcindor's value and impact as a player.

In obtaining Alcindor, Wooden had captured lightning in a bottle. He was too good, too threatening, and other teams began to lash out unfairly. The fans, too, took sides against him. He made it seem too easy, and his relaxed, controlled style on the court hinted at relaxation beyond that expected of an athlete participating in a varsity competition. Alcindor's great height and his skill at working free under the basket did indeed simplify the act of shooting. In that debut against USC he made twenty-three of thirty-two field goal attempts, sank ten of fourteen foul shots, cleared both boards with methodical movement, looked for the open man, and passed with amazing skill.

The other teams were stumped. They had tried the man-to-man defense, which proved an abysmal failure. They experimented with a double-team defense, fronting and backing him, and that failed just as quickly. A collapsing zone, with three and sometimes four men falling back into the center lane, showed some promise but at too great a cost. It slowed Alcindor but freed three deadly shooters. So they got down to elbows and knees, fists and hips, tripping, shoving, and insulting. They tried to goad Alcindor into a burst of rage, hoping he would become unnerved and angry. It did not work.

The physical stuff worked all too well. Lew was hitting the floor with all the regularity of a punchy prize fighter. He was shoved and stepped on. He took a finger in the eye or a forearm across the throat. He was kicked and scratched, harassed far beyond what is allowed under the rules of the game. But still he scored and rebounded, and continued to play excellent defense.

"I had been used to that kind of basketball in New York," he said. "I didn't want to show my anger because I've always been a little afraid of losing my cool. I kind of expected it to happen, even before it did. Really, there's nothing you can do about it. I was bruised and scratched and after a particularly rough game I ached. But it was part of it. They didn't know what else to do. I didn't think they were right, and I hated to play that kind of game. I tried not to. I just tried to do what was okay and hope for the refs to spot the fouls."

Victory followed victory as UCLA toured the country to play the best of the nation's teams. Duke fell on successive nights. Also defeated were Houston, Washington State, Oregon, California, Notre Dame, and Northwestern. As his prowess grew and he seemed invincible, racism entered the picture. Opponents tried to prod him into fights by using every word known to pluck the pride of a black man. That failed too, for Lew had long since been inured to that. His father had given him that distasteful segment of his education and had prepared him for the insults and the slurs.

"I never even heard that jive," he said. "It went right past me. You can find people all over the country who use that stuff, but it doesn't do what they want it to. It hurts to know that people do it, but I didn't let it affect my game."

Hate mail and crank calls never stopped the UCLA team or its leader. The season reached its last weeks and UCLA, still unbeaten, was growing stronger, feeding on each victim and preparing for the NCAA tournament and the first of what would become three consecutive national championships.

Meanwhile, a subtle change had come over Lew Alcindor. He did not again hit the heights of his fifty-six point night, for once he found the defenses were keyed to stop him, he refused to force his shots, refused to waste scoring opportunities. "I don't mind passing," he said. "The job here is to win. It would be selfish of me to force a shot if any of the team was clear. I'll take my shots if I can, but that doesn't happen very often. So I pass off and we make easy baskets, and I try to do my best in rebounding, because that leads to more easy scoring chances."

Wooden, too, found himself commenting on Alcindor's attitude. "He doesn't hesitate to pass, and he realizes his value to the team when he does. He is an unselfish player who does what has to be done to get another win. But he is very reassuring on your side when they begin catching up, because he always seems to have his best games under pressure. When we absolutely need a basket or a rebound, or when it becomes crucial to stop the other team from scoring, Lewis finds a way to do it. The others admire him for this. He could easily have taken to dominating the offense, and who would have been able to stop him if he wanted to score fifty or sixty points every game? But it's better this way. Much better."

UCLA cavorted through the regional qualifying rounds of the tournament and easily reached the final round-of-four in Louisville, Kentucky. The other teams were Houston, Dayton, and North Carolina. UCLA drew Houston in the semifinal, and the spectators anticipated a clash between Alcindor and Houston's All-America center, the 6'9" Elvin "Big E" Hayes.

Hayes was sky-high for the game, determined to prove his superiority over Lew. In his own way, one would assume, he achieved that goal. He outscored Alcindor by six points, 25–19, and he had twenty-four rebounds to Lew's twenty. But UCLA won, 73–58.

The final was against Dayton, whose Flyers had upset North Carolina by utilizing a sensible patterned offense, a

tenacious defense, and the all-around brilliance of 6'4"
forward Donny May, another All-America who was to be
drafted by the Knicks. Alcindor was the key to Dayton's
chances for an upset. If he could be held to a reasonable
output, the Flyers were confident of handling the other
four starters. But it did not work; nor was there any reason for the theory suddenly to prove workable at this late
date. Alcindor was not going to be held to any reasonable
limitations. He blocked shots with ease; those he did not
block he caused to be launched artificially and as a result,
missed. Who can forget the image of May driving to the
basket, having neatly beaten his man, and, seeing Alcindor towering above him, releasing the ball at a too-high
arc, hoping for a bank-and-roll off the top of the backboard, over the immense wing span of this one-man defense.

May missed six such shots, otherwise automatic baskets, and it was this faculty of being able to dominate that
enabled Alcindor to take his teammates to the title,
79–64. UCLA had its national championship and an unbeaten season that had now stretched to thirty-one games.
That was Lew Alcindor's first year in varsity basketball.

He had, of course, been named to every All-America
team selected. Not many sophomores had managed to
evoke such unanimous praise and recognition. Only Wilt,
Oscar Robertson, and maybe Jerry Lucas and Bill Bradley had made an equal impact on the world of collegiate
basketball in their sophomore seasons, but none of them
showed the rapid progress that Alcindor offered.

For that matter, none of them had ever precipitated a
change in the rules, but that is what Lew did. During the
summer, while he was renewing New York acquaintances
and taking in as much of his beloved jazz as possible, the
College Basketball Rules Committee had met. Many
coaches were terrified of Alcindor's effect on the game,

and they began searching for methods by which to curtail him.

Raising the basket was no answer, for the smaller players would operate under more of a disadvantage than Alcindor. Attempting to make it easy for the rest by lowering the basket was ridiculous, since it would cause scores to skyrocket. Widening the lane, which had been tried in the past, would not limit the scope of Lew's ability.

Banning the dunk shot would. At least, they reasoned, he would not be able to deposit the ball in the basket without some semblance of a shot. It might not stop him, but it would make him work harder for his points and, perhaps more importantly, it would take away from the fans the spectacle of Alcindor stuffing a ball through a metal rim with childish ease.

What the Rules Committee really did was to remove one of the most dramatic, crowd-pleasing shots from the repertoire of many players besides Lew. The dunk shot, or the stuff shot, had become a mark of distinction among those short enough to accomplish the feat only if they were blessed with superior leaping ability and precise body control.

To see a player 6'2" soar into the air and slam the ball down into the basket was a sight many fans openly applauded and gleefully anticipated. But Alcindor had made the shot methodical, too easy, a part of the arsenal with which he psychologically intimidated other teams. The Rules Committee said it was done to prevent injury and circumvent the many broken rims and backboards, but they and everyone else knew it was a step taken to cut down Alcindor.

"It was for Alcindor, not because of any injuries," said a player on another super college team. "There are guys a foot shorter than Lew who can stuff, and they took it away from all of us. It was all right for all the years before, but now it was no good. It just didn't make any sense."

Thus, when Lew began his junior year at UCLA, it was with the new, somewhat disturbing, and absolutely unnecessary restriction against the dunk shot.

But Alcindor was correct in assuming that the change in the rules would not limit his productivity. That junior season rolled along with the same ease as had the sophomore season. Victory seemed automatic, and the winning streak approached astronomical proportions. It had reached forty-seven games when the first major test was offered to the band of UCLA hotshots.

The villain was Houston. More specifically, it was Elvin Hayes.

Ever since the defeat in the semifinal game at Louisville the year before, both the Cougars' coach, Guy Lewis, and his star, The Big E, had boasted of what they would do in the rematch, a regularly scheduled season game to be played before more than fifty thousand fanatic Texas fans in the Houston Astrodome.

"He's not really all that good, you know," Hayes told reporters about Alcindor. "He's not especially strong, and he can be moved out from under the boards. And I'm not so sure he likes to play defense much. I think we can take care of him, and I think we can beat UCLA. Lew just isn't aggressive enough, and he stands around too much."

The Cougars had won seventeen straight since their tournament setback, and they were billed as the number two team in the country by the Associated Press and United Press International. Clearly, then, the winner of this one would be able to claim the top spot for the rest of the season.

The date was Jan. 20, 1968, and a national television hookup had been arranged through the use of 153 independent stations from Maine to California, from Florida to Alaska. But more had entered the picture, and it had added a note of suspense to the classic confrontation. Just eight days earlier, in a game with the University of California, a freak minor accident had resulted in a scratched eyeball suffered by Alcindor. It was on a UCLA shot that missed, and in the subsequent battle for the elusive rebound, a finger poked Lew's eye. "I don't know whose it was," he said. "These things happen all the time. I'm certain no one meant to do it. Heck, you can't aim a finger that good. It was just one of those things."

Undoubtedly. But "just one of those things" had caused Alcindor to suffer from double vision and headaches. He was terrified that he would be forced to miss the Houston game, and so he sat out the two games played in the intervening time, meaningless clashes with Portland and Stanford that UCLA's bench could have won. For three days he lay in the darkness of his room, eyes bandaged, trying to speed up the healing process.

Unfortunately, it did not come around as quickly as he had hoped. He had not practiced for a week, not even taken a shot, when the team left for Houston. Lew felt he had to play, for the grudge match that Hayes had instigated had touched Lew's pride, and he wanted very badly to have a good night.

It was not to be. Not only had Alcindor missed practice for a week, but he had been unable to do any running. He was out of condition; his timing was rusty, and his shooting was faulty. He still had the double vision but, to his credit, he never used it as an excuse for what might happen. But he was playing with a severe handicap, and Wooden realized it. "I do not want to alibi," he said prior to the game. "Lew will play. You all know he injured his eye last week, and I do not know how well he may play. He has not been practicing with us, but he wants to play and he will."

He did. But he did not play well, and, as a result, neither did UCLA. Hayes, meanwhile, sensing an advantage and feeling the momentum of the game shift to Houston, took full advantage. He scored from every angle and from everywhere on the court. He played tough defense, blocking shots viciously. He rebounded strongly off both backboards, exerting himself until he produced a terrific game.

"I had been so high for that one," he said, "I think I would have cried if we had lost. It was all I could think of, that game, from the time I found out we had the chance to play them again."

The UCLA depth, however, was so incredibly stubborn that the Bruins almost won without Alcindor's usual big game. The final score was 71–69, and it was Hayes who had accounted for the final margin of victory with two pressure foul shots with twenty-eight seconds left to play. After they had been made, UCLA had one more chance, but Mike Warren deflected a pass out of bounds, and Houston was able to consume the final precious seconds, with George Reynolds dribbling away the clock. The streak had been snapped. Houston had toppled the colossus, and Hayes had been the weapon. He scored thirty-nine points (to Lew's fifteen), and he collected fifteen rebounds while Alcindor managed just twelve. Moreover, Lew had made just four of eighteen field goal attempts, and he was booed off the court by the delirious hometown partisans at the conclusion of the game.

The UCLA players were dejected, but Alcindor was more crushed than any of them. "It was my fault," he said quietly, in the stillness of the team's dressing room. "I was lousy." Not once did he mention his injured eye and subsequent faulty vision as a possible excuse.

But he did issue a flat pronouncement that was to ring true with the quality of the competitor he had become. "I wish Houston luck," he said, "because I don't want to see any other team beat them until we get our chance. I figure that will come in the NCAA tournament again, and I just hope they make it that far."

Houston did make it. So did UCLA. Both teams continued their seasons undefeated. So on March 22, 1968, in the Los Angeles Sports Arena, the two teams once again took the court to compete for the championship.

It was a semifinal round game, but the country's fans knew that this one was for the championship. This one was going to produce the national king.

Houston never had a chance. Alcindor's eye had healed, and his shooting had returned. His defensive magic had surged back stronger than before, for now he was a young man with a mission. The mission's name was Elvin Hayes, and the mission's objective was to stop him.

UCLA came out in a storm of offense and a full-court zone press defense that stifled the Cougars. Hayes scored only five points in each half, missed shots from the same places he had hit from against Alcindor in Houston, and the final score, 101–69, in no way indicated the extent of the actual beating Houston took that night. Wooden might have had a winning score of 150 points had he let the starters finish, but he chose not to embarrass Houston or coach Lewis any more than necessary.

As expected, the final game for the championship was a laugh. North Carolina, which provided the opposition, quickly joined the expanding list of UCLA's victims. UCLA won its second consecutive NCAA prize, 78–55, with Alcindor scoring thirty-four points and eliciting such praise as "he is the greatest player who ever played this game" from North Carolina's coach Dean Smith.

The record stood at 59–1 for two varsity seasons. Twice in succession Lew had been named to the All-American teams. Twice in a row he had been named the NCAA Tournament's Most Valuable Player. Twice in a row he had been the dominant factor in a game of major importance played under nearly professional pressure.

There was nothing dramatic or spectacular about his senior season. Lew just did his thing, and UCLA did its thing, and the victories continued. One defeat, a maddening slowdown ruse planned and executed by rival USC, did not overly sadden the Bruins. They had become complacent with winning, and all generally agreed a loss was beneficial in the long run and that it would provide impetus in their drive for an unprecedented third straight NCAA title.

There had been an extended trip home for Alcindor when UCLA participated in and won the Eastern College Athletic Conference's Holiday Festival in Madison Square Garden. In winning, the Bruins were lethargic. They took the best shots of several exceptional teams and batted them back with casual ease. Clearly, UCLA was the cream of the country, and even a victory over St. John's in the final game plus the Most Valuable Player Award of the tournament did not impress Alcindor. He had begun thinking about the NBA. He had just about run out of challenges as a college superstar.

The NCAA championship was, naturally, in the cards. A brief scare in a regional game with Drake (UCLA won, 85–82) was overcome, and the Bruins manhandled Purdue, a Big Ten representative with high-scoring Rick Mount in the lineup. Alcindor's last college outing resulted in thirty-seven points and twenty rebounds, and his college career was finished.

He had averaged 26.4 points for 88 varsity games, and he still holds the NCAA record for field goal accuracy, having made 943 of 1,476 shots, a miraculous 63.9 percent.

"When I went to UCLA," he said, somewhat bitterly, "people expected me to do the impossible. They predicted we would win the NCAA championship each year because I was going to be so good. Well, it wasn't automatic, and I kind of resented all the pressure. But people are naturally that way, and I was really relieved when the college part of my career was finished. If I had things to do all over again, I don't know how I would have changed them. I wanted a college education, and the way for me to do it was to play. I just wish people would have left me alone, or at least treated me with the same degree of attention they treated the rest of the team. There were many times when I resented being different."

Lew Alcindor was twenty-one years old, and he had learned a great deal. But the education he received in his classes was just surface material. He learned to deal with every form of abuse, including racial attacks. "I don't know how he took it," said teammate Heitz. "We all felt for him, but there was nothing we could do. If people are that way, it's going to take a lot more than a couple of basketball games to change them. I'm sure Lew was glad his college days were over. At least he could look forward to being paid for the abuse he took."

Even coach Wooden was relieved that the Age of Alcindor had passed. "It was a great thrill to have known a person like Lew," he said, "and it was thrilling to have won all those games and those three championships and every tournament we entered. But I'll tell you this. It will be nice to coach to win rather than to coach not to lose. There was a lot of pressure on everybody. It was artificial, strained, for all of us. But Lew's great talent made it so, far beyond the point at which he could control it. I wish him all the luck in the world as a professional, and I don't think he has yet reached his peak. He'll learn faster with the best in the world to play against, and as he gets stronger, he'll become even more intimidating. I think one might safely say he is going to be the best this game has ever known."

It did not take very long for the speculation to begin.

There were, in the spring of 1969, two professional leagues—the proven, established NBA and the upstart ABA, which had nothing in the way of prestige but a great deal in the way of available spending money. To land a prize such as Alcindor would have given the ABA instant success, a lucrative television contract, immediate notoriety, and automatic parity with the NBA. The teams and the league's administration were frantic to sign this skyscraping ticket salesman, while the NBA was determined to keep him out of the new league, to preserve its own future and to deny the ABA a chance to grow and prosper.

The bidding began, and had Lew himself not enforced a ceiling on the offers, there is no calculating the fairytale figures the bids might have reached. On March 19, 1969, J. Walter Kennedy, the commissioner of the NBA, a quiet, reserved man who lived in Connecticut and took the daily commuter trains to the league offices in New York, arose with the realization that the first step in the attempt to land Lew Alcindor was to take place that afternoon.

Two teams were in the running for the right to negotiate with Lew, the Milwaukee Bucks and the Phoenix Suns. Each franchise was one year old and, as a result, had met the accustomed fate of all expansion clubs. They had experienced horrendous first seasons.

According to the NBA system, the last place clubs in each division, Eastern and Western, flip a coin to determine which will draft first. It is a time-honored method by which the weakest teams are given a chance to strengthen themselves, since all clubs draft in reverse order of their season records.

No mystery existed as to the first player who would be selected. Each team was desperate to land Alcindor. He represented improvement far beyond the wildest hopes of the owners of the teams. His presence on the team would mean contention in the divisional pennant races, and he would be an instant box office hit.

By a prearranged schedule, Kennedy was to set up a long-distance telephone hookup including the offices of the Bucks and the offices of the Suns. Wes Pavalon picked up the ringing phone and heard Kennedy say: "Hello, Wes. This is Walt Kennedy in New York. I have Dick Bloch [of the Suns] on the other end of this line." Pavalon, chairman of the board of the Milwaukee team, exchanged pleasantries with Bloch, and Kennedy outlined the ground rules for this million-dollar coin flip.

"Gentlemen," he said, "I am going to put the receiver down on my desk. Then I will flip this coin in the air, catch it in my right hand, and put it on the back of my left hand. I have Connie Maroselli and Helen-Marie Burns of my staff here as witnesses."

Phoenix had been given the Bucks' consent to call the toss, since the Suns had conducted a survey of their fans, asking them to write in their preference of "heads" or "tails" if given the choice. Jerry Colangelo, the Suns' general manager, announced that the preponderance of votes had been for "heads," so Bloch made a public statement announcing that decision. Pavalon had graciously agreed to allow him the privilege of making the call.

The coin lay on Kennedy's left hand as he picked up the receiver again.

"It's tails," he said bluntly, and immediately a wild celebration broke out in the Bucks' crowded offices. Pavalon burst onto the phone and yelled: "We've got him. We've got him."

In Phoenix, Bloch listened to the melee, waiting for an interval in the deafening noise. Pavalon, realizing Bloch was still on, picked up the phone and heard Bloch say, in a deeply disappointed voice, "I hate to say it, Wes, but congratulations."

Meanwhile, the ABA had conducted a soul-searching among its teams, and it had been agreed that the New York Nets, based in Lew's home city, offered the greatest inducement to the homesick superstar. Indeed, Alcindor had privately expressed a preference for this arrangement, saying, "The NBA has better basketball, but the ABA has New York, and the Knicks won't be low enough to draft me." Indeed, the Knicks had finished much too well to be even close to it. No other team would have considered trading those rights, for it would mean establishing a decade-long dynasty in Madison Square Garden, since the Knicks were already so very rich in talent.

The owner of the Nets was trucking magnate Arthur Brown, and although the other teams in the league offered to help him raise sufficient cash, he declined. "I can handle it myself," he said wisely, "and if I do, I will not owe anything to anyone."

The line was drawn now. The Bucks in the NBA and the Nets in the ABA went to war. But Alcindor forced an uneasy peace on these two factions before they had begun to sling rocks and sticks and cashiers' checks. "I will accept only one offer from each team," he informed, through his two advisors, Californians Sam Gilbert and Ralph Shapiro. "I will accept one offer, and then I will choose the better one with the help of my advisors. I will not engage in any extended negotiating that would lead to a long and drawn out newspaper circus, and I do not want to make enemies of anyone."

Alcindor set a date for these offers to be handed down,

far enough in the future to allow reasonable time for computing such astronomical figures and yet close enough so that he would miss none of the all-important training time. He arranged to meet in a New York hotel with the Bucks and then to go to the nearby apartment of Brown.

The Bucks were first. Their offer was for five years, and it represented a $1.4 million package including stock, cash, insurance policies, and the like. It was a record figure, an incredible one, and Lew Alcindor, amazingly, took it in stride.

Then it was the Nets' turn. Brown, accompanied by then ABA commissioner George Mikan, a one-time NBA superstar and the first of the truly great bigmen, was also offering a five-year arrangement. He had in his hands a cashier's check for $1 million, which he placed face up on a desk. "That's my offer," he said, "and it comes to $200,000 a year for five years, guaranteed."

He did not have to break it down for Lew, and Lew did not have to say any more than "It does not meet the Milwaukee offer, Mr. Brown. That's under the figure they offered me."

"I can't go any higher," Brown said.

Lew turned to Shapiro and Gilbert. "That's it, then," he said. "I'm in the NBA."

The ABA owners, infuriated at Brown's failure to outbid the rival NBA, tried to reopen negotiations a few days later, and they presented a package that amounted to a breathtaking figure of $3.25 million. But Alcindor had informed Kennedy and Pavalon of his decision. He had given his word. "I'm sorry," he told the ABA, "but we made an agreement and I lived up to it. I'm sorry you didn't make this offer first, but I have made a promise to the NBA, and I won't go back on it now."

Alcindor was truly sorry, for he had expressed the private hope that the Nets would come up with the better offer. "If I had to choose," he said, "and if the money was not a consideration, I would pick the Nets because of New York. I would love to play in New York. It's my home city and my favorite city. But the Knicks couldn't get the rights to me, and I was ready to settle for the ABA's brand of basketball, hoping it would improve. I was sort of disappointed."

With Alcindor's presence drawing in more and more of the highly rated college stars, the ABA would surely have improved. But Alcindor had made a pact with the two teams, and he felt bound to live by it.

So, on October 18, 1969, Lew Alcindor, wearing a brown and white Milwaukee uniform with the number thirty-three on its back and front, trotted out onto the court and played his first professional game, the Bucks' home and season opener against Detroit. It was going to be a remarkable season.

In their first year of play, the Bucks had won just twenty-seven games. With Lew, they won fifty-six. In their first year, the Bucks had finished a dismal last in the Eastern Division. With Lew, they were second, just four games behind the juggernaut that had been assembled in New York. Alcindor averaged 28.8 points per game, second only to the fabled Jerry West's 31.2 figure for the Los Angeles Lakers. He took down an average of 14.5 rebounds, third behind Elvin Hayes' 16.9 and Wes Unseld's 16.7. His 51.8 field goal percentage was seventh in the league, and the 3,534 minutes he played trailed only San Diego's Hayes. Lew registered season highs of 51 points against Seattle, 27 rebounds, 20 free throws, 21 field goals, and nine assists. He was a superstar the first time around.

But he was more. He was, as a veteran player expressed it, "an entirely new force in pro basketball. He has no idea how good he can be."

Alcindor's professional coach was Larry Costello, a former NBA star known for his direct and hard-headed coaching techniques. Nothing fancy or elaborately contrived entered into the Milwaukee playbook, for Costello coached the same way he had played—hard and fast, basic and simple, and to win.

"When we saw what a talent Lew had," he stated at midpoint in the rookie season, "we would have been foolish to design anything more than a center offense. I wanted Lew to play as much as he could for two reasons. First, because we didn't have a quality backup for him, he had to strengthen himself, to build up his stamina, because someone as overpowering as Alcindor should play all the time, or at least until the game is decided. That leads to the second reason. Who would want to have a man like Alcindor available and not utilize him? He's a game winner. I've heard some criticism of my offense, which involves getting the ball to Lew as often as possible. But didn't the Cleveland Browns hand off to Jimmy Brown whenever they could? Didn't the Dodgers start Sandy Koufax whenever they needed a big game? I would be remiss in my obligations to this team and to the fans and to Mr. Pavalon if I didn't get as much out of Lew as I possibly can. He has the opportunity to become something unique in this game, and it is up to us to see that he develops as quickly as possible."

And so Lew Alcindor underwent the rigors of his first NBA schedule, a sadist's delight that calls for eighty-two regular season games before the playoffs begin, *after* a pre-season schedule of games played for the revenue to defray expenses and the vital training time.

"The one thing that worried me about pro ball," Alcindor says, "was the roughness. It would be silly to say there isn't a great deal of contact under those backboards, and I guess I got my share of it because, in the beginning, they had to find out how much I would stand for, how much I could take. I wondered if I was physically strong enough to handle it, because I had never played that long a season and never against such strong centers. I'm tall, but I'm not very heavy (230 pounds), and I wondered, under the stress of playing game after game, if I would lose even more weight.

"At first, I considered a weight-lifting program to build me up, but then I watched the strong centers, the men like Wilt, and I discovered they were built different. I would lose my agility if I played too heavy. Then I used to watch Bill Russell play for the Celtics. I had been a fan of his for years, and it occurred to me that he was built the same way I was, kind of long and lean. I decided that if he could do it, if he could put up with the contact, I could too. But I'll tell you, it's rough. It's always rough in this league."

It quickly became apparent that a little roughness was necessary if other teams were to stand a chance against the suddenly vitalized Bucks. The bigmen in the NBA, the proud veterans, were all of the same opinion: "The kid is too good to handle by ourselves. We need some help."

The defenses began to give evidence of this concern. Forwards moved inside to "front" Alcindor when the Bucks had the ball. A man stationed behind him did all he could to make Lew's move to the basket difficult. Guards set up in what was thought to be the passing lanes, hoping to deflect balls thrown into the pivot where Alcindor hovered, waiting ominously.

But nothing really worked. The chief proponent of

"just play him and hope for the best" was Reed of the Knicks, a burly 6'10" player who gained much experience and agility as a forward at a time when towering 7' Walt Bellamy was the New York center. Reed has the moves of a forward with more than usual strength and force, and he alone proved capable of playing Alcindor one-on-one. The fact that he outplayed Lew in many of their key matches was not a slap at the rookie but a tribute to Reed's determination and savvy. Yet even Willis speaks of Alcindor as someone special, someone soon to emerge as much more than another top-notch center.

"In his first season," Reed explains, "Lew just wasn't sure of what was expected of him. Oh sure, he knew he was supposed to score a lot of points and grab a lot of rebounds and block shots. We all know that. But when he got the ball, he didn't react immediately to the basket. Sometimes he'd take a few bounces, sometimes use a few fakes he didn't really need. He would pass up an easy shot to use that fall away jumper. But each time we played Milwaukee he was better. You could see progress, real progress, each game. It's not so much now a question of his improving any more as it is of his learning what he does not have to do.

"When he gets that high pass, if he's anywhere near the basket, all he should have to do is go toward it and release his shot. There's no way a man can block his shots without fouling him. When he puts the ball on the floor, he's asking to have it batted away. I would like to get a lot of basketball played in a short time, because when this kid gets it all together, I don't think I want to put up with that job. No one will be able to stop him. The rest of us are just centers. He's a whole team."

The other bigmen in the league spoke of Alcindor in equally glowing terms. Chamberlain, Unseld, Thurmond, and Hayes added their praise to Alcindor's performance as a rookie. So, too, did the coaches. "You really don't expect to stop him," said New York's Red Holzman. "What you want is to keep him to his forty points. But even that is getting to be a big job."

Alcindor's first meeting with Wilt Chamberlain represented to the rookie a high point of sorts. He had always admired the legendary Laker, and he had a natural and healthy curiosity about how he would do against Wilt. According to Chamberlain, Lew came out very well indeed.

"He's good," said the bearded giant, "and he'll get to be very good. He isn't as strong as he'll become, and he doesn't know all the tricks of the NBA centers, but how could he? He hasn't had the time to learn them. I thought he was as good as any rookie center I've ever played against. No, I guess he was better, because on one or two occasions he absolutely fooled me. He just beat me, went past me, and got the basket, all in the confined space of maybe three or four feet under the basket. It was surprising, and I'm sure he didn't know for sure what it was he did. He has great natural ability."

As the season progressed, the Bucks improved with each game, for as Alcindor became more familiar with his job, the job became easier for him and tougher for his opponents.

In other seasons, Milwaukee might have finished first in the Eastern Division. But the Knicks were super, especially so at the start of that 1969–1970 campaign. When they won twenty-three of their first twenty-four games, including an NBA record of eighteen straight, they all but locked up first place. It was left to the rest of the teams to chase them home, and Lew Alcindor's Milwaukee Bucks quickly proved to be the best of the rest.

Baltimore dragged in third with a 50–32 mark and Philadelphia, barely able to finish over .500 (at 42–40), nailed down the fourth and final playoff spot in the East. In the West, the order of finish for the teams eligible for playoff was Atlanta, Los Angeles, Chicago, and Phoenix.

Without much effort, Milwaukee dispatched the 76ers, and the Knicks edged Baltimore in seven games. Thus the classic confrontation occurred in the Eastern playoff finals, with Alcindor and Reed as central figures. The winner of this series, said those who followed the sport, had the best chance of emerging as the NBA king, because the Lakers and the Hawks, who had reached the Western finals, could not match either of the Eastern powers in depth and defense.

The Lakers had Chamberlain for only the first twelve games of the season before he tore knee ligaments and was forced to the sidelines for the rest of the campaign. He had returned for the playoffs, but he was a limping, much slower facsimile of what he once had been.

In the playoffs, however, Alcindor was faced with a determined Reed, who knew all the moves, who had learned all the tricks from all the best pro centers, and this was the year the Knicks were going to win their first league championship. Lew dominated, of course, as he always does, but Reed played him well, and the rest of the Bucks were no match at all for the fired-up Knicks.

Although the playoff series lasted only five games, flashes of Lew Alcindor at his best came through with regularity. He was in the Eastern Division playoff finals, and still he showed no more emotion on the court than ever. He trotted up and down in that peculiar loping stride, arms hanging limply at his sides, and he turned on at will the fury of basketball at its best.

In the first game, played in New York against the team he had watched as a youngster, the team he had always dreamed of playing for, he scored thirty-five against Reed's twenty-four. He took down fifteen rebounds to

Reed's twelve. But somehow, Reed managed to be there for the key shots, the clutch rebounds, and for the crucial block when only a block could save the Knicks.

New York won, and Alcindor was typically downcast. "I'll just have to play better," he said. "I missed too many shots tonight, and I can't keep doing that if we are going to win." Characteristically, he shouldered the burden for the entire team.

He did shoot better the next night, making sixteen of twenty-five field goal tries, finishing with thirty-eight points, twenty-three rebounds, and eleven assists. It was more basketball in one game than most bigmen put together, especially as rookies. But once again a bit of misfortune befell the awesome giant.

With just fifty-two seconds remaining on the clock, he missed two free throws with New York ahead, 110–109. The Knicks won 112–111 and Lew was treated to a full dose of those unique New York boo-birds who populate Madison Square Garden.

The Bucks won the next game, in Milwaukee, but lost the final two and disbanded for the season. They watched with some comfort as the Knicks took the Lakers in seven games, the last three with little or no help from Reed, who had torn a hip muscle in the fourth game. Alcindor was in Los Angeles for the games played there, and he was not cheering for the Knicks.

"Isn't it all right for you to be a Knicks fan again now that the season is over?" a reporter teased.

Lew smiled. "No, I'm not a Knicks fan any more," he said, "but if you have to lose the playoffs, you'd like to have the team that beat you win it all. It makes a little more sense that way, makes you feel just a little bit better. The Knicks beat us, which means they had to be very, very good. So I want them to beat the Lakers, because if they do I'll be able to feel we're the second best team. Next year? We'll be the best then."

If this sounds like the end of the Lew Alcindor story, it is not. It is only the beginning, for Lew has become, in a short time, the most respected and the most productive superstar in a long history of NBA superstars, as the 1970–1971 season demonstrated.

He came out of high school in New York City and set out across the country to Los Angeles. He sought out the pressures in California, listened to what the UCLA fans demanded of him, and then delivered it. He became the most widely heralded, eagerly sought collegian in more than a decade. When he was ready for the pros, he very nearly took a young, upstart league into national prominence before he changed his mind and signed on with the establishment.

He almost catapulted a two-year-old franchise to an NBA championship, and he fulfilled every standard, passed every test, met every challenge set down by the most wildly optimistic NBA fan. He rebounded in the toughest league in the world, the grim battlefields under the NBA backboards.

He proved he could shoot and score against any of the great centers. In his short time as a pro, he converted Chamberlain, Thurmond, Reed, Hayes, and Unseld. He made them see what he could do, and dared them to stop him. He took their best shots, and he came up a winner. There were times, which became more frequent and more habitual, when they could not begin to prevent it.

His soaring leap for a rebound was rivaled only by his leap with a stuff shot. His graceful reach to block a shot was matched only by his unselfish attitude toward passing, toward hitting the open man.

They say Lew Alcindor has made it because he is so

tall. There are others who claim he has made it in spite of his height. Somewhere between those poles lies the truth.

He is tall. But he is also good.

The story of Lew Alcindor, the rookie who made it big when they expected nothing less, is a dramatic story for that very reason.

2

Calvin Murphy

CALVIN Murphy has lived with his particular problem for a long time, yet he blinks wonderingly when it is referred to as a problem.

His height, you see, is less than what one might expect for a man who is a star basketball player. Calvin Murphy is exactly 5'9".

Well, 5'9" is not really *that* short. It is only three inches shy of six feet, that barrier above which people are referred to as tall. There are a great many outstanding basketball players who are 5'9" or shorter.

You may see them perform on any playground, in any industrial league, on several semipro teams.

But in the National Basketball Association?

Well, that's Calvin's problem.

"No problem," says the diminutive San Diego Rockets guard, "no problem at all. There are things a person my size can do that bigger players cannot. I'd love to be a lot taller. Heck, I'd like to be seven feet tall. But I'm not, and since there isn't a thing I can do about it, I'm not about to start worrying. I'm short for basketball, but I can make do."

Make do, indeed. Calvin has shaken the NBA mightily. In his 1970–1971 rookie season, he literally terrorized those unfortunate NBA guards who had reached that awkward height of 6'4" and 6'5". They tried to guard him, and he mysteriously slipped past them. They tried to dribble around him, and he suddenly materialized to slap the ball away. When they attempted to take him underneath the basket, where they could use their height to shoot over him, one of two things happened. They either lost the ball to a flick of his lightning fast hands or Calvin's avowed "bodyguard," 6'10" San Diego center Elvin Hayes, lammed their shots back at their heads.

Calvin has reshaped the offensive theories of the game. He has given hope to other "shrimps" of the country who never even thought of trying. In fact, he has caused some imaginative and far-sighted coaches to discuss the advantages of being "caught short" in the land of the giants.

His own coach, former NBA great Alex Hannum, speaks admiringly of Calvin's value to the Rockets, a recent expansion franchise which can use all the help it can get.

It was at the insistence of Hannum and San Diego's general manager Pete Newell that Murphy was drafted as high as he was, at the start of the second round. Hannum wanted him, and Newell, a former college basketball coach with glowing credentials, concurred. Both men agreed that Calvin was somehow different and that despite his stature he would blossom into an NBA star.

"We scouted him pretty thoroughly," Hannum said. "Remember, he was an All-America selection three years running at Niagara, so we had plenty of opportunities to see him and to talk to other people who had seen him. You know what the most striking factor in coaching him was? Well, it's kind of difficult to understand, but when a man watched him in a game, he began to forget that Calvin was only 5'9". You know, he did everything a guard has to do. He is a fine shooter, deadly accurate from almost anywhere. He is a top defensive player. He has speed we couldn't believe. He passes beautifully, and he is a leader who can run the team. We needed a guy like Calvin, and the fact that he is 5'9" never stood in our way. I firmly believe Calvin will become a star in the NBA."

Others who passed judgment on this firecracker from Norwalk, Connecticut, included Bill Russell, former Boston Celtic center. "Calvin Murphy belongs in the NBA," said Bill. "He will be an outstanding pro player. Not everything revolves around the size of the player. He has to want to excel. He has to have many skills aside from just possessing sufficient height. He has to be determined, he has to hustle, and he has to be a smart player. Calvin has all of those ingredients. 5'9"? What does it matter? He'll make it."

Still, it was felt that Murphy would stand a better chance of acquiring fame and fortune if he had chosen to play in the American Basketball Association, the newer league in which the overall quality of competition is not as high as in the NBA, and there is a need for competent guards.

But those who know Calvin Murphy knew that these very reasons precluded the ABA's chances of landing him. He wants to be the best. He demands to face the most rigid challenges. He would not be satisfied with the big-fish-in-the-small-pond way of life.

"I want to be classified as a great ballplayer," he says seriously. "I know I can take the physical punishment in the NBA, and that's the biggest adjustment I can see in playing with the pros. Naturally, there will be an attempt to take me under the basket because of my height, but there are two ways I can think of to stop that. First, I have to play good defense, to stop the other man from getting underneath easily. Second is Elvin Hayes. He's going to be back there to knock down a lot of shots."

From his first days at Niagara, in upstate New York, after a high school career climaxed by All-America selections for three straight seasons, Calvin Murphy began to think about professional basketball. He considered the possibility while others scoffed. He discussed it rationally while friends offered many reasons for expecting disappointment. He explained how he would have to approach a professional career, how he would have to attack the odds against him, but others snickered and doubted.

Sitting at a sports banquet one day, Murphy, then a junior, spoke with a man about his future in basketball.

"I would like to try pro ball," he said. "I don't think I want to settle for the ABA, at least not until it has been proved to me and I can't make it in the NBA. To be honest, I think I have what it takes. I know I can shoot, and I know I have speed. There has never been any doubt about my ball-handling, and I think I can play defense. Heck, I've covered bigger men all my life. Maybe they weren't as good as the bigger NBA guards, but I wasn't as good then, either. If I'm not drafted, I'll try to get a tryout as a free agent.

"I think I'll be playing in the NBA. At least, I know I want it badly. I've thought about it all my life. My height? Well, I'm short. I can't hide that or explain it away. But I can jump well, and that tends to make me taller strictly in a basketball sense. If I shoot well from the outside, I'll disrupt the defenses, because somebody will have to come out to me. And then I can pass inside, underneath. But I want to prove I can play. I hope I get the opportunity."

There was no star more exciting in collegiate basketball in the three seasons played during the years 1967–1970 than Calvin Murphy, the three-time All-America at Niagara. There have been few as exciting since his graduation, and there were few prior to the time when he began hypnotizing crowds and demoralizing opponents.

To study the college player that was Calvin Murphy is to discover the dramatic growth process of a *scorer* developing into a complete *player*. He entered college as a shooter, a dazzlingly accurate point-maker, an adept passer and ball-handler. He often drew officials' whistles for walking violations, because they were unable to believe any man could move the ball as fast as he did, because they refused to accept the fact that his famed "half-step" dribble, with the ball going through his legs in time to the pace of his trotting, could be achieved legally. However, one national magazine published a high-speed photo sequence proving that Calvin's between-the-legs and behind-the-back dribbles were legal and did not constitute the violation of carrying the ball an extra step.

But gradually Calvin became a master of the finer points of the game.

"In my first season," he explains, "I was interested in scoring. I always had been able to make the shots, and that's really all I worked on in high school. I loved to score. I loved making those long jumpers and those twisting lay-ups. I suppose part of it was because I felt I had to prove I was as good as the bigger kids, but it was also a case of doing the things that turned on the fans. I dug that applause. I really did.

"So when I started playing freshman and varsity ball for Niagara, I became involved in the scoring part of the game much more than in the defense and in the playmaking. And in freshman ball we could win if I scored a bunch of points. It took me two full seasons to discover that I wasn't helping myself as much as I could, and that I was nowhere near as valuable to the team as I might have been."

Nevertheless, Calvin found time to establish every single Niagara scoring record, in addition to setting several team records, all of which still stand.

The sixty-eight points he scored against Syracuse on December 7, 1968, is the all-time school record for a single game. He made a record twenty-four field goals that night. The twenty-one foul shots he made against Columbia on January 16, 1969 (out of twenty-two attempts), constitutes another record. He also holds the single season scoring record (916 points), the most field goals in one season (337), the most foul shots in one season (242), and the highest varsity three-season scoring average (33.1).

Needless to say, his career point total of 2,548 is by far the highest in Niagara history. He reached the 1,000 mark early in his junior season during the twenty-seventh varsity game in which he had competed. On March 8, 1969, he became the highest scorer in the school's history when he scored point number 1,683. Point number 2,000 came on Dec. 30, 1969, against Oklahoma City University.

All this was accomplished after a superlative freshman season, in which he averaged 48.9 points for nineteen games, making 364 of 719 shots (50.6 percent) and 201 of 240 free throws (83.7 percent).

During his varsity career, Calvin established arena records on seven courts across the country, including the Philadelphia Palestra mark of fifty-two points; the Buffalo Memorial Auditorium record of forty-eight points; the Syracuse University Manley Fieldhouse mark of fifty; the Niagara Student Center record of sixty-eight; the Jersey City Armory standard of fifty; the Columbia University record of forty-seven; and the Detroit Tournament record of forty-one points.

But as Calvin continued to play, he discovered other facets of his talent. He became adept at passing to the open man rather than launching those wondrous thirty-foot jumpers. He was the nation's second highest scorer in his sophomore season, averaging 38.2 points per game. But that was when he still felt scoring was the only desired result of basketball, when he chose to accept the challenge issued by another high-scoring sophomore sensation, LSU's Pete Maravich.

Significantly, his scoring average dropped solidly in each of his next two seasons, but his overall worth increased with as much impact. He averaged 32.4 points per game in his junior year and 29.4 as a senior, but it was in that final season that he truly became the complete player.

A host of respected veteran coaches rushed to praise him and to offer encouragement for the professional career he had already indicated he wanted.

Villanova's Jack Kraft, after watching helplessly while Murphy tormented his Wildcats for three seasons, acknowledged Calvin's greatness. "He is the best shooter I have ever seen," said Kraft. "Pro, college, or high school, in all my years of watching this game, he is the best. No ifs, ands, or buts about it. I don't think there is a defense in existence that can stop him. He does more with the ball than any player has a right to do. There's no chance the pros will pass him up, and I don't think a chance exists that he can fail."

Murphy's own coach, Frank Layden, who took over at the helm of the Purple Eagles in 1968–1969, was understandably one-viewed about Calvin's prospects. "He'll be even better in the pros than he was in the college game," Frank said. "He's been defensed by three men throughout his entire college career. In the pros the zone is outlawed, which means Cal can go one-on-one. And I don't think there's a man alive who can contain him in that kind of a situation. He'll win any single match-up."

Other compliments poured in, in part probably as a result of relief that Calvin could no longer harass college coaches.

Penn State's Johnny Bach insisted that Calvin was "the greatest college basketball player since Oscar Robertson" and then added "but he did more, because he was much shorter than Robertson and had other problems to overcome."

Lou Carnesecca, then the head coach at St. John's in New York and now the head coach—general manager of the New York Nets of the American Basketball Association, was equally impressed with Calvin's defense. "When he's playing defense, if you open your mouth, he'll steal your teeth. The kid seems to have 9′ arms, a dozen of 'em. He's a joy to watch, unless you have to coach against him. Then he becomes a nightmare."

Larry Weise of St. Bonaventure offered more. "Calvin is so quick it is almost impossible to stop him. He comes down the court at full speed, suddenly stops, and then releases that soft jumper. He's a tremendous shooter, and remember, too, that he is a terrific ball-handler. As a pro, I don't think he can miss making it big."

Rutgers' then coach Bill Foster pointed to Murphy's leaping abilities as one of the many assets of a pro career. "Cal can make it. He gets up there really high, and that evens up the disadvantage he would have in a standing-still match-up. He's always moving, always jumping. He has a fine outside shot, and he's as quick as a cat. When we played Niagara, we never thought of Murphy as 'only' 5′9″. We talked about him as impossible to stop, regard-

less of his height. With him, the height didn't really matter."

The pro scouts, even as far back as Cal's sophomore
season, were equally taken with this pint-sized superstar.
Paul Seymour of the Detroit Pistons was one of the first
to go on record praising Calvin as a potential professional.

"He'll make it in pro ball. He has speed, and he can
shoot. He probably will be picked on the first round, because when a kid can do all the things Calvin can, it almost doesn't matter how tall he is. There have been a lot
of great small pros, and if there haven't been any lately,
it's because there haven't been any good enough, not because the game has phased them out. Calvin Murphy is
good enough. You can bank on it."

Eddie Donovan, as fine a judge of talent as any man in
the game, has been the general manager of the New York
Knicks of the NBA, and he now occupies the same position with the expansionist Buffalo Braves. Donovan was
another to speak well of Murphy.

"There is always room for talent in our league, and
Calvin has great talent. He's a great shooter and a fine
passer, and don't forget that he can play tough defense. I
don't think anybody has ruled him out. In fact, several
people have spoken with me about him, and they already
feel he can easily make it."

Clearly, men who earn their living appraising and
coaching basketball talent could not all be wrong. Calvin
was on his way, despite the stature that outsiders felt
would hinder his professional efforts.

Murphy is a showman. His flair for entertainment on
the hardwood may not permeate his game to the extent
that Pete Maravich spiced his performances, but Murphy
is pleased when his dexterity with a basketball draws applause and attention.

During his years at Niagara, he developed a pre-game warmup drill that was as delightful to the paying customers as was his basketball expertise. Accompanied by the background music from such mod sounds as James Brown, the Jackson Five, the Iseley Brothers, and the 103rd Street Rhythm Band, Calvin would move out to the foul line and begin firing off passes to teammates who were cutting for the basket.

But the pass itself, often thrown blindly but accurately, was the end result of some remarkable ball-handling. He would feed, with total accuracy, from behind his back, around his neck, off his elbows and heels, and even on a ricochet off a third teammate. Interspersed, of course, was fancy dribbling, spinning the ball on the end of his index finger, and, for a final flourish, the spectacle of a 5'9" guard bounding toward the basket, soaring up and up, and slamming the ball down through the rim for a stuff shot, the likes of which are usually the province of far taller men.

The crowds loved it. They went wild, stamped their feet, cheered, and yelled. It was a pleasant way to start a game.

"I used to worry that people would think I was grandstanding—a hot dog," Calvin remembers. "But it was the other guys on the team who asked me to do it. Also, I think the fans liked to see it. I was always able to do those things with the ball, and when I used them in practice the guys seemed to pick up. I used to practice all alone when I was a kid and couldn't find company, and I got a kick out of working on my 'tricks' as well as on the other parts of the game. Yes, I call them tricks, and I don't expect I'll use them in a pro game. That really would be showing off. But the dribbles behind and back and through the legs are real weapons. I can get past a man by doing those things. I don't think of them as tricks at all. They are part of my game, and I'm happy I can do them. They help."

Calvin Murphy was born May 9, 1948, in Norwalk, Connecticut. It was a slum life to which Calvin was introduced, and he grew up with the ghetto kids, many of whom ran into serious trouble before the idea of educational advancement occurred to them.

This, too, is a part of him, and he wants to be able to do something about it, something about helping the other kids who must still live this half-life. But he is not like the athletes who say they want to help and then conveniently forget about it when the chance presents itself. Calvin is dedicated, and he does help. And he feels he can do much more after he has established his NBA identity.

"I want to work with kids before they get into trouble," he says. "When I was growing up there was a man, Mr. Leroy Vaughn, who ran our community center in Norwalk. He was the kind of person who really cared. He not only helped us but he also told us when we were wrong. It was men like him who kept me out of trouble."

Calvin wants to go back into the ghetto, where he can be of most service. The sort of job he has in mind can best be termed "trouble shooter." Perhaps its definition lies somewhere between the duties of a policeman and a social worker, between harsh authority and too-close camaraderie.

"The easiest way to reach these kids," he says, "is through sports. The main problem is to get them to stop thinking that you're a policeman or some sort of cat who has to have a job and is just going through the motions, just mouthing words that don't really mean anything. These kids just can't associate with police authority. I wouldn't want to wear a uniform, because that might negate everything I hope to do. But those kids are quick to spot a phony, too. You really have to be sincere.

"I mean, it's not so much for me to tell them that drugs and crime are bad, because either they know it's bad and don't care, or there is no other alternative in their minds. The thing I can show them, and I am physical proof of what I'll say, is that they can get out the right way. They can get to college, and they can learn a trade, and they can become members of a greater community, not just the ghetto street community. If it wasn't for me and basketball getting together, I don't know what I would be today, or what I would be doing.

"There were plenty of chances to get involved in something wrong, but I had basketball. If I couldn't find anybody to shoot with, I'd go to the playgrounds and shoot by myself. I'd play little games in my mind, or I'd practice a particular shot, and I'd see if I could make a certain number of consecutive jump shots or foul shots. I guess a lot of my free time as a boy was spent playing basketball. I have to think it helped me stay straight, and it provided me with all this."

To date, "all this" includes the scholarship to Niagara, after an intense period of pressure for the High School All-America from Norwalk High. Jim Maloney, who was Niagara's head coach when Calvin was a high school senior, said he spent so much time in Norwalk he expected to have to pay taxes. "But wasn't he worth it?" Maloney once asked. "Just watching him go in those high school games was worth it."

"All this" includes also the three-time All-America honors at Niagara, where Calvin developed from a shooter into a team player, from a scorer into a dedicated leader.

Finally, "all this" includes the San Diego Rockets, who decided to take the chance with a kid who was too short, and who now consider themselves lucky to have been so farsighted.

William T. Guthrie, the sports editor of the New Haven *Journal-Courier,* talks of Calvin's high school career in the words of a man who spent much time watching the youngster go from boy to man.

"The biggest thing in his favor," Guthrie begins, "was quickness. I mean, everything he did he did quickly. He looked like a machine running on transistor batteries and jammed in high gear. He'd go through warmups at top speed, he'd play the whole game at top speed, and I suspect he even toweled himself off in the shower at top speed.

"Sometimes, when you are involved in covering high school athletics, you see a kid clearly superior, and you start to wonder if the provincial nature of the job can affect your judgment. You know, if I went around the country talking up a kid who is 5'9" and plays for a high school in Norwalk, Connecticut, who would take me seriously? But all of us could see what Calvin was capable of. He was as fine an athlete as I have ever seen, and I have covered many professional teams, too. There was something special about him. He seemed so much more mature than the kids his own age. He'd make moves that the good college player couldn't make, and they were moves that came from pure instinct. You could tell he didn't have to concentrate on making those fakes. He didn't have to think about it—he just did it."

And so, after the prep days in Norwalk, during which time he was named twice to high school All-America teams, Calvin selected Niagara from the hundreds of major colleges vying for his favor.

"Why Niagara? Well," he explains, "I liked the school. It has a good educational reputation. My mother and I had decided that an education was, after all, the most important thing. Also, it wasn't too far away, so I could come home weekends and holidays, times when I felt I had to be home for a while."

Calvin bristles noticeably when it is suggested that Niagara offered a better chance at national repute for a 5'9" basketball player who might have been lost in the shuffle of a larger university with higher pressure on athletics.

"No," he says, "I chose Niagara for its educational value. Basketball has always been a big sport up there. It is smack in the middle of a basketball area with built-in college rivalries [St. Bonaventure, Canisius, Buffalo University, Gannon College, and others] and the caliber of basketball is as good there as anywhere in the country. My reasons for choosing Niagara were based solely on education. Sure, basketball provided me with a scholarship, and I don't think we would have been able to afford college if not for the scholarship, but I tried not to let that influence my decision. A lot of places offered me scholarships. But I have never been sorry I chose Niagara."

Nevertheless, there was some report of discontent after Calvin's freshman season and again after his sophomore season. The rumors began to circulate that Calvin was going to transfer to another university, either Houston or Marquette. Murphy was annoyed. "I'm staying here," he said in response to several telephone queries. "I have never considered a transfer. I'm happy here, I'm pleased to be playing basketball here, and I have no intention of going anywhere else. Absolutely not."

Meanwhile, the other teams, the ones that had to play Niagara, were spending most of their time dreaming up defenses to stop him. Much as opponents of UCLA had to arrive at some method of curtailing the game-breaking qualities of Lew Alcindor, Calvin presented a similar problem.

"It wasn't so much trying to stop him as it was trying to limit his output," said Rutgers' Bill Foster. "There was really no way to stop him. He was going to score no matter what you did, but if you bothered him enough, maybe he'd get only twenty points instead of thirty-five and the difference in what he scored usually meant the game. We never really wanted to put anyone on him man-to-man, because it just wouldn't have worked. He was too quick. He got past his man, and then he was free and clear.

"What we tried to do was never let him get that free. If he beat the first man in the zone, we'd try to have a second ready to pick him up. We never gave him the middle because of those drives he liked to make, because it would have been too easy for him to disrupt the entire defense. We tried double-teaming and triple-teaming. We went to sliding zones, and we tried the box-and-one. Other coaches tried putting bigger men on him, but it didn't work that well.

"Maybe he'd have more trouble shooting over them, but he could hurt the bigger man with his quickness. You know, we never came up with anything that really worked. If Calvin had a bad night against you, people would congratulate the coach for setting up a great defense. But it was just because he was missing. There really was no way to stop him in college. Also, it was risky to put too many people on him, because he was such a great passer he'd find that open man all night. I'm not so sure I'd like to try to stop him again. Maybe, though, if I had a Calvin Murphy on my side, I could do it, because he was so great on defense he might have stopped anyone."

The sophomore season, Calvin's highest scoring year (point total and average), was his last played under Jim Maloney. During January of that season, Maloney announced his intention to resign at the conclusion of the schedule, for business and personal reasons. Shortly thereafter, Niagara announced the hiring of Frank Layden, a former Purple Eagle basketball star, then working as the head coach of Adelphi-Suffolk (now Dowling) College on Long Island.

Niagara had already sent ten alumni on to the pros: Larry Costello, now head coach of the Milwaukee Bucks, Manny Leaks, Al Butler, Boo Ellis, Tom Hemans, Bo Erias, Charlie Hoxie, Ed Fleming, Zeke Sinicola, and Joe Smyth. But now Calvin was getting closer and closer to the pro status he so intensely wanted, and when Layden took over, they talked about it.

Layden is a friendly, intelligent man. He wages a constant battle with his temper on the court and with his waistline off the court. But he knows basketball as well as any coach—better than most—and he knew when he took the job at Nagara there might be difficulties with the rest of the team if he concentrated too hard on building and increasing Calvin Murphy's talent.

"We never held a formal meeting," he says, "but we talked informally with all the players from time to time. We discussed various ways of winning, because even in Calvin's sophomore season, with as many points as he was able to score, the team was under .500 (12–13). We decided that our best weapon was Calvin, and it became obvious that if we wanted to win, there were three things we had to do.

"We had to play tough defense, we had to do a better job on rebounding, and we had to get the ball to Calvin. But it worked in another way, too. By working harder, by moving without the ball, by getting position, and by making the right moves, the guys were finding themselves free for easy shots. The defenses were so scared about covering Cal that they forgot to cover a lot of the other people, and with Cal being such a fine passer, we started getting the easy points. He'd feed, they'd go up, and we'd get two points. Those were points that Calvin was as responsible for as if he had made one of those incredible thirty-foot jumpers.

"It began taking hold, I would say, about midway through my first year there. We didn't have a very good record for the season (11–13), but we closed strong. We knew we were much better than at the start. Some time in the middle of that year, Calvin suddenly changed. He became better, too, because he became all-around.

"He was always a marvelous shooter, of course, and he always had the talent for playing sticky defense. But he began to see that if he passed to the kids who were getting clear, he would accomplish two things. First, they would get us the easy baskets. Second, the defenses would really be in a panic then, and they'd have to lay back a little in defending him, looking for his passes underneath. That gave him easier shots. I think we put it all together in his senior year. I was as proud of those kids as I could be. They proved that with hard work and by plugging at something, they could win a lot of games against bigger and more talented teams."

Calvin's senior season, as Layden so accurately describes it, was excellent. The Purple Eagles finished at 22–7 overall, their best since the 1953–1954 season. The team was considered good enough, nationally, to be ranked seventeenth in the Associated Press polls. Niagara was tendered an at-large bid in the prestigious NCAA (National Collegiate Athletic Association) tournament, and the Purple Eagles upset mighty Penn in their first game, 79–69. Calvin Murphy was the game's high scorer, with thirty-five points.

But then Niagara wandered into competition too overpowering, for this was, after all, their first experience with post-season tournament basketball. In the Eastern Regional finals, at the University of Maryland's Cole Fieldhouse, Villanova (98–73) and North Carolina State (108–88) defeated the Purple Eagles.

"We learned a great deal from that tournament," Layden says. "We saw that we could win, that we had the necessary ability to become a winning team. But we also saw how much Calvin meant to us. He was just superb in the tournament, as he was all season, and we knew it was going to be very difficult playing without him. I'll always be sorry that for his sake the last two games he played were not winning ones. He deserved better, but on the other hand, we never would have gone to any tournament without him, and so I hope he saw that the whole season was, in a way, a tribute to his capabilities."

The college career of Calvin Murphy was finished, but he was not yet ready to leave school. He was intent upon receiving his degree, an accomplishment too many other athletes seem ready to abandon once their athletic eligibility has run out. Also, he chose to confer occasionally with coach Layden, for he sought advice on how to handle the professional offers, should they come. He sought direction.

"What I really didn't know," he says now, "was which league I would be better off choosing. I knew the really top flight players were in the NBA, but I also knew there was no one as small as I. The ABA seemed to be a nice league, with its emphasis on the guards. I was well aware of the three-point rule (on baskets made from outside a twenty-five-foot circle). I knew my shots were all from nearly that far away, and I guessed I would be able to score a bundle in the ABA. But, well, it's hard for me to explain. I had always wanted to see if I was as good as the best. From the time I had begun to follow basketball, the NBA was always there and had all the great stars. I don't mean to demean the ABA because it's new. I'm sure it will be as good as any league, but all the players I had sort of idolized were in the NBA. Guys like Oscar and Earl Monroe and Jerry West. You know.

"I had heard from both leagues, and both of them said they were hopeful I would play for them. The offers were about the same as far as the money was concerned, but I guess I had unconsciously made up my mind about the NBA. I wanted to try it there."

The only real advice Layden could offer was a probing question leveled at his star player.

"Do you feel you're good enough to play in the NBA, Cal?" he asked.

Murphy smiled, answered that he thought he was, and discovered that he had made his decision. "If you really think you can make it," Layden added, "why not go for the NBA? Nobody will think any less of you if you fail."

So Murphy had made up his mind. It was done well in advance of the date when both teams would announce their draft choices. "I didn't want to cause any bad feelings," Calvin says, "and I didn't want to get involved in a bidding war. When I had decided I was going to go to the NBA, I made my feelings public."

Thus the San Diego Rockets, who made Calvin their second-round choice, were the fortunate ones. Since they had finished last in their division and as a result had been awarded the top choice in each round, Calvin was actually the 18th player in the country to be drafted by the NBA—not bad for a shrimp. But the ABA, not willing to lose a chance to negotiate with him should he be cut, drafted him anyway. The Pittsburgh team (then the Pipers, now the Condors) drafted Calvin as its first-round selection. The Pipers, as well as many of the people who navigate the perimeter of pro basketball, felt there was a better than average chance that Calvin would not make it. After all, there was the problem of his height.

But when Calvin reported to the Rockets' training

camp, he immediately made his presence felt. Proving once again that he could play with the bigger boys, Cal put on a show of basketball that caused San Diego coach Alex Hannum to glow with anticipation.

Playing in the team's rookie camp, he scored ninety-nine points in three games against rookies from other NBA teams. He dazzled the crowds with his passing and his ability to control the ball, and he forced Elvin Hayes to calculate the number of "basket passes" he might expect when playing with this little wizard.

"What I saw was a kid who could get to be a superstar in the NBA," Hayes told a reporter shortly after. Hayes, being a superstar himself, should know. "He has more moves than anyone I've seen come into this league," Elvin continued. "I don't think he'll have any trouble getting used to playing up here. He has speed and moves, and he can pass and shoot as well as anyone. Will they try to take him underneath? Well, I guess they'll try it, but that won't win games. Doing that forces an offense to stand around and wait for the man to use his height advantage, but if the guy keeps missing, or if a guy like me blocks those shots, they'll just have to get off it. This game is too fast to start doing things like that. You have that clock to keep you going, you know."

Hannum was more specific in his appraisal of Murphy's potential.

"He has the speed to pick up an offense," said the 6'7" 220-pound former Southern Cal All-America and NBA All-Star. "He always seems to be moving, but it appears that he knows just what he's doing and just where he's going every minute. He has more innate basketball sense than any rookie I've seen in a long time. He fires up a team just by his hustling. It's almost a case of the other guys not wanting to look as if they're loafing by comparison. Calvin is a great shooter, and the way he jumps indicates he won't be bothered by being shorter than the rest of them. I'll have no hesitation in using him, playing him extensively, even starting him. It's as easy for a short guy as it is for a tall one to make it in this league, if he has the necessary talent. And Calvin has it."

One of the other professional coaches to have witnessed this debut was Bob Cousy, once considered to be the finest "small man" in the NBA and, at 6′2″, the integral member of a legendary team, the winning Boston Celtics of the 1950s and 1960s.

"With determination," Cousy said, "Murphy will be a superstar in this league." Cousy is now the head coach of the Cincinnati Royals and he, perhaps more than anyone, knows the problems and the advantages of a small man in a giants' world.

"It's much easier for a small man to break into the NBA now than it was when I started in 1950," he explained. "Then there only were eight teams. Now there are seventeen and if the merger with the ABA goes through, there could be as many as twenty-eight. So on the strength of numbers alone, Calvin should make it.

"The problem of his lack of height has been greatly exaggerated. If he does have a problem, it may be in coordinating his talents with those of his teammates. Some kids coming out of college try to do it all by themselves, but I understand that in his last couple of years in college Calvin concentrated on playing team ball. He'll have no trouble on defense provided he picks up at the three-quarter point on the court," Cousy continued.

"But if he gets lazy and picks up at the top of the key, well, then his man will have him at a disadvantage. A fellow like Murphy will have to press."

And so he does, but not because it was suggested to him. Calvin always did and he always will. He knows no other way to play.

"I have to keep moving," he explains. "It's important to me to bother the other guys on defense as much as I can. You'll notice that the top defensive guards in the league, guys like Walt Frazier of the Knicks, are always pestering the man with the ball. You just can't sit back and wait for them to dribble up to you any more, because they're so quick they'll dribble right past you if you're just standing around."

As far as scoring big with the pros, Calvin feels it has less meaning for him and less value to the team than playing good defense and concentrating on feeding the bigger men.

This is part of the theory he turned to when still a junior at Niagara. At that time, after scoring nearly forty points a game as a sophomore, he explained his new outlook this way:

"We play teams with their defenses set to stop me, and those teams should have to pay the consequences by losing. I think everybody on this team has made sacrifices to individual glory for a team effort. That's the difference, and that's what I have to do too.

"Most of the teams we've faced," he continued, speaking about his senior year, "have found out this is not a one-man club. The other two Niagara seasons I played were with players who had equal ability, but now we are much more of a team. Almost every club we play is bigger physically, but my teammates do a good job off the boards and we have good teamwork. Every man on this club has hustled all the way. It's a question of determination. If you want it badly, you'll work to get it. We wanted it.

"I know teams are trying to stop me, and if that's what they think will work, fine. It weakens their defense in other places. I'm not the only one on this team who can put the ball in the basket. I know I could score more if I shot more, but what good would it do if we lost? No good. And that's the reason I'm passing more."

As a sophomore, Calvin shot an average of 32.2 times per game, less frequently than the 40.3 times he shot as a freshman. Yet as a junior that figure dropped to 29.2 and, in his senior season, it dropped dramatically to 23.9 shots. And now that he is a professional on the way to stardom, his new theory has not changed.

Today Calvin Murphy stands in a locker room dressed in the green, gold, and white garb of the San Diego Rockets and talks about his career.

"I didn't expect to have an insurmountable amount of trouble in the pros," he says candidly. "I knew what I could do. It was a question of getting enough of an opportunity to show the coach and the other players, so that they would have more confidence in me. Playing pro basketball is a great deal different than playing any other kind, but not so different that it isn't possible to adjust. The first thing to do is to figure out what is expected of you. For instance, I knew that there was no way the team was going to depend on me to score a lot of points. That would be foolish. At Niagara, I was in that position, but that was a completely different situation.

"Up here, everyone is a good shooter. I never realized how many great ones there were, really, until I started playing. It seems everybody has a great jump shot, and almost no one misses many foul shots. They can all shoot quickly from any point on the court. Their fakes and the drives are sensational. I guess one of the surprising things I learned is that big men are almost as quick as the small ones, especially with the ball in their hands.

"Everybody is attuned to the basket. Everybody thinks offense."

There, perhaps, is evidence of what Calvin Murphy's role is in the game. He is one of the best defensive players in the game. His quickness and outright speed can be matched by few men, and the attitude with which he continually approaches defense makes him that much better and more effective.

He does not oversimplify his goals. He does not irritate his questioners, as so many other athletes do, by making obvious statements such as "defense is designed to stop the other man from scoring." No one can totally shackle an NBA shooter. No one can prevent an outside man from scoring, unless that man is suffering a bad night.

The object of defense, more realistically, is to make a player take shots he does not ordinarily want to take—to make him force his good shots, to make him shoot hurriedly, to keep him off-balance. In short, the object of defense, NBA-style, is harassment.

There are several methods used by the professional that are not allowed in collegiate competition. Hand-guarding is one of them, and no one has mastered this particular technique better than the New York Knicks veteran guard Dick Barnett. The job he did on Jerry West in the 1970 championship playoffs was a tribute to Barnett's dedication, and even then the Los Angeles Lakers' legendary scorer finished the seven-game series as the top point producer.

Hand-guarding is the practice of maintaining constant contact with your opponent by use of a hand. His jersey, his back, his elbow, and his hip are targets for the ever-present pressure of a hand. Clutching or holding in such a defense is not permissible, but the constant pressure of the hand on the offensive player can accomplish much. Indeed, most of its value seems to lie in the psychological effect it has on the shooter. The hand becomes an annoyance, a distraction, and it takes away from the total concentration needed to get clear enough to shoot the good shots.

No one can deny that there is far more physical contact in professional basketball than in college competition and that officials have closed their eyes to such defense. To call each occasion of contact, however incidental, would be unworkable and would extend the games to a ridiculous length of time. Playing defense against the finest shooters in the world is difficult enough, and any small edges the defensive players cares to explore are regarded with stoic tolerance by the referees, as long as these "edges" do not get out of hand.

But Calvin Murphy does not employ the hand-guarding technique of defense, nor does he go out of his way to find contact. "I would be the loser in that kind of a game," he says.

Calvin's defense is, even at this early point in his career, truly unique. It is constant motion, continuous darting and slapping at the ball, a studied exercise in harassment that gets under the skin of the most poised veterans.

"I keep moving," he says. "I keep trying for the ball. If you let a man take the ball upcourt without bothering him, you are already at a disadvantage. Because once he reaches his end, there are too many things he can do to hurt you. He can lead you into a blind pick and get free for an easy shot. He can pass off to an open teammate. He can drive past you, or he can feint a drive and drop back for a jump shot. The idea is to bother him in the backcourt, to try to interfere with his dribble, to make him worry more about where you are than where the ball is."

The theory sounds simple enough, and when given the quickness, the speed, and the intelligence of Calvin Murphy, it really is easily executed. But not many of the pros can do it, a fact which has become clear to the fans who have grown to respect this little dynamo from Niagara.

"I don't think I'll ever block anybody's shot," he says.

"At least, not once they get up there. But if I can bother them enough, maybe they won't get the time to take that kind of a shot. Then I'll know I'm playing defense as well as I can. Defense is a team thing. All the players have to be involved in it. Look how far the Knicks went with their team defense. It's just great, and I hope ours will be as good soon."

But the other players and coaches around the league dispute Calvin's thoughts on his style of defense.

"I've seen him block shots," says Bill Fitch, coach of the hapless Cleveland Cavaliers. "He just looks short, but he's really a 6′9″ player wearing the disguise of a man 5′9″. I've seldom seen anyone with his jumping ability. He just seems to go higher and higher and then hang around for a while up there. I'll tell you, he's a treat to watch, but not when you're a coach, and he's working against your team."

Dick McGuire, former head coach of the Knicks and now their chief talent scout (he switched jobs with Red Holzman midway through the 1967–1968 season), was one of the first to predict pro stardom for Calvin.

"I know he's only 5′9″," McGuire said after witnessing a Niagara game in Madison Square Garden. "But he's a unique 5′9″. First of all, he can leap. He can do it consistently well, and he times it perfectly. That makes him taller, in a basketball sense. Then there is his ball-handling. I don't think I can remember any man who was as adept at ball-handling in college. Maybe Bob Cousy. Maybe Oscar. But no one was any better than this kid. And he's a scorer. I don't care who is guarding him, he'll be able to score. He's so quick he only needs a split second and he can get free. Put all that in with his defense, which is great, and I don't see how he can miss. He'll play in the NBA, and he'll play well enough to star."

Other scouts were equally impressed: Boston's Red

Auerbach, Jerry Colangelo of Phoenix, Detroit's Paul Seymour and Earl Lloyd, and Baltimore's Bob Ferry foresaw success for Calvin in their league.

"I'll take him," said Auerbach, the general manager and the former head coach of the Celtics, before the draft. "I need a big center badly, but if Murphy is still there on the second round, he'll be my next pick." (He was not, of course, available, having gone to the Rockets.)

Murphy entered the NBA as its smallest player since the middle 1950s, when Slater Martin, also at 5'9", was an All-League guard. But Calvin's job was far more difficult, since Martin was much closer then to the average height of the NBA in that era. Today, 5'9" is miniscule, and if you doubt that statement, look forward to your first sight of Murphy walking downcourt with Milwaukee's Lew Alcindor. There is a difference of eighteen inches there, and most of the NBA players would be closer in size to Alcindor than to Murphy.

Calvin's season started on the road, since the Rockets' first four regularly scheduled games were in Baltimore, Philadelphia, Chicago, and Buffalo. He had, of course, been the sensation of summer camp, and he had scored those ninety-nine points in three rookie games. But now they were finished playing for fun, now it was to count.

The first game, on October 14, was against the Bullets. Calvin scored seventeen points, stole four passes, deflected several more, and blocked two shots. He was the immediate star of the show. The crowd loved every minute of his performance, and he was awarded with a long ovation when he finished.

Game number two was in Philadelphia, and against the powerful 76ers Calvin scored seventeen points again. Again the crowd went wild. There, too, he was rewarded with boisterous applause.

When the Rockets reached Buffalo, fan support hit its peak. Despite the fact that he scored only six points, this was the biggest moment yet in his pro career. He had "come home" to the same Memorial Auditorium where he had accomplished so much as a collegian, where the fans were much more familiar with Calvin Murphy than they were with their new NBA team, the Braves.

More than ten thousand were in attendance, and when the introductions were made, Calvin received the loudest and most sustained cheer of any of the players. They cheered his every step. They rooted for him even when he was attempting to defeat the home team. They absolutely loved him, and he was terribly disappointed with his sub-par performance.

"I was tight," he admitted later, "and I was pressing. I was coming back to my college town and my college fans, and I think I tried too hard to be good. I wanted to have my best game for those people, and I started to make mistakes. I never really felt loose, and I have to feel that way to play my best."

There would be more appearances against the Braves of Buffalo, but now Calvin had to prepare himself for the home opener, October 20, against the Phoenix Suns. Again, he had a mediocre night as far as points are concerned. He managed to score only eight, but one of the field goals, a long, soft jumper, came late in the game and led to a one-point victory, a fact that alleviated some of the disappointment during post-game discussions.

"I'm glad that's over," he said. "I have been thinking about the first one in San Diego for a long time. I didn't do well, but I'm glad it's over. I can stop being nervous now."

And he did. From then on, the points began to flow with greater frequency from Calvin Murphy, and fans across the league flocked to his support. He scored thirty-six against Chicago on January 5, 1971, and received a hero's salute from the partisan home crowd. Several times since then he has reached past the thirty-point barrier, and by midseason of his rookie year he was averaging fifteen points per game.

"It's a phenomenon," says Nick Curran, the NBA's Director of Public Relations. "Whenever and wherever he plays, people are curious to see what he can do, to see what this little guy is all about. He has that baby face, and he looks so small and helpless out on the court that they take to him, identify with him. Basketball is the kind of game almost everybody has played, and since most people are much closer to Cal's height, or even shorter, they never even considered going any further with the game beyond school. Now they can see one of their own making it big against all those extraordinarily large people. He's an underdog, you see, and people always root for the underdog."

For the Rockets, an expansion team with a great deal of improvement needed before they can compete for championships, the two most difficult teams to play in the late 1960s and the 1970s were the New York Knicks and the Milwaukee Bucks, the cream of the NBA. Staying close against these two powers became an achievement meritorious in itself.

Early in the 1970–1971 season, the Rockets journeyed across country to play in New York. It was on October 29, and the Knicks were prohibitive favorites. It was suspected that Red Holtzman's team viewed the game as a warm-up for some tough ones to be faced in the near future. Elvin Hayes had scored forty points the night before against the expansion Cavaliers, and it was felt he would be the only functional Rocket on the court.

New Yorkers turned out in abundance, as usual, but not only because they were fans of the highest quality who were savoring the realization of a world championship team after twenty-five years of bitter frustration. They were also intrigued with the prospect of Calvin Murphy, having seen a great deal of him during his collegiate appearances in the Garden and on television.

And Calvin did not let them down. He entered the game in the second quarter and at once became the whirling dervish he always tries to be. He swatted away passes and dribbles. He scored. He acted as a playmaker for a team that had started to stand around watching the Knicks operate with their usual aplomb.

He fed Hayes with the accuracy of a master passer, and he even blocked a few shots taken by the highly distressed Dick Barnett. The Knicks ultimately won the game, but it was neither easy nor relaxing, and it was definitely not a warm-up game. The Knicks had to work for it, and when it was finally done, their fans paid special tribute to Calvin.

Later, Calvin talked about his first game in New York, which is always an important time for a rookie, especially for one who grew up in the metropolitan area of New York and spent his youth at least well aware of, if not actively rooting for, the Knicks.

"Sure, I had a lot of friends and relatives in the stands," he smiled, "and if they were before, I don't think they're Knicks fans any more.

"But seriously, this was a big game for me. I've played in the Garden before, and it always seemed special. But after being drafted and making the team in the NBA, coming back to New York was even more rewarding. I was flattered to hear so much applause. I'm not sure I can say I really deserved it, because we lost. But it was nice to know people care. I think we have a fine team, a team that soon will be a winning one. I hope I play a part in that.

"What do I think of the Knicks? They're great. They are the champions, and I guess that means they are the best in the NBA. But it's hard to pick out any one team and call it the best because there are so many good players and so many good teams. That, I think, is the toughest thing to get used to, that any man you cover can beat you, that any team you play can win. I was thrilled to play in the Garden, and it was great to be playing there in front of these people, but it would have been nicer if we had won the game. That's what this is all about, isn't it? You get paid to win."

If that sounds too mercenary, too much like a cold and callous professional, it must be taken in the light of what Calvin Murphy feels he owes basketball.

"This game took me out of a ghetto life," he insists, although there are those who feel he would have made it out anyway. "I owe almost everything to basketball. I was able to earn a college education, and that will always be with me, something that no one can take away. I know I can hurt myself, tear up a knee or something, and not be able to play again. But I'll still have my college education, and I know I'll be able to to do something useful and productive with it."

Uppermost in Calvin's ambitions, of course, is that youth work. He wants to provide an escape route for others like him from the grip of poverty and ignorance, to give them a chance to become educated and enlightened human beings.

Calvin's mother Ina was influential in getting Calvin interested not only in athletics but also in the problems and needs of ghetto children. She was a great athlete in her own right, playing for the Bomberettes, a women's basketball team representing Carver Center, a Negro settlement house in Norwalk.

Calvin's consideration of small children has always

been obvious, from the time he played on the Norwalk Biddie League team right up to now, when he enters or leaves a professional arena in the company of those towering giants he calls his teammates. He tries never to refuse a request for an autograph.

"Kids in the slum areas," Murphy says, "do not trust most of the people who honestly try to help them. They do not like uniforms. They can be reached by the guys they know, and slum kids follow sports figures more closely than they follow any others. So I feel I have an obligation to try to show them the way out. I was lucky because I found basketball, but there are thousands of good kids who will not be able to use sports as their ticket to a constructive life. I can help them. I can be a bridge."

Calvin has arranged with San Diego Police Chief Don Rued to work out some of his ideas while the season is underway. He is serious about this, and he is just as determined to make it his life's work—after basketball, that is.

"I suppose coaching kids would be one way," he says, "but maybe that would be too restrictive. That way I would only come into contact with the athletes. I want to give all of them a chance, not just the players. People are people, whatever they do, and they all deserve the opportunity to better themselves."

Clearly, then, Calvin is using basketball for the greater good of all. The road to success in the sport, he hopes, will lead to a more meaningful purpose once he is through with the game.

"If I make a name for myself," he says, too modest to realize he has done so already, "I will be more recognizable to kids all over the country. Then I can use myself as an example, to show them what an education can do, what determination can do. There is hope for all kids, wherever they live, whatever their situations are. I would like to be able to show them this, to prove it to them."

Meanwhile, until the time when his worthwhile goals can be fulfilled, Calvin Murphy will continue to thrill basketball fans across the country. He has accomplished much in the time since he found basketball, and there is much still to be done.

No one doubts he will become a superstar in the NBA. No one doubts his abilities as a basketball player of wide-ranging skills. He has achieved a goal that many felt was far beyond his reach.

"I've never known a man to work any harder to excel," says his coach, Alex Hannum. "He drives himself all the time. He has more stamina and more ambition than any rookie I've seen. It has been a rewarding experience working with him, and he is the kind who makes you proud to be his coach. He can't help but be a great success."

There were some people, however, who had always believed in him, who never thought that this half-pint kid from Connecticut would fail.

"It's all inside a person," he says. "It is all there, if you want to do it badly enough. You just have to be willing to work for it."

If the opposition is going to minimize the threat posed by young Calvin Murphy, they will have to work for it, too. But their chances of success are minimal at best, for Calvin will never stop working to improve.

3

Pete Maravich

Lew Alcindor accomplishes his goal by means of great height and greater talent. Calvin Murphy accomplishes his with determination and talent. But Pete Maravich seems to work with magic, mirrors, and hypnotism. Surely there can be no other explanation possible for the miracles he works with a basketball in his hands.

This intense, complex, and dedicated young man, a 6'5", 190-pound blade of tightly wound steel, who looks undernourished and overworked and seems to need two good weeks in a nice fresh-air camp, revolutionized the game of basketball when, with his dad, he descended on the Baton Rouge, Louisiana, campus of Louisiana State University. The older Maravich, Press, was the head coach at LSU; his son, Pete, was the star. Sadly, enough controversy resulted from that situation to fill another book.

Pistol Pete set every major record for a single game, a

season, and a career in the annals of the NCAA's statistical bureau. He reached levels of scoring that were considered impossible and then surpassed his own records.

As a sophomore, Maravich averaged 43.8 points per game, scoring a total of 1,138 and winning the national scoring championship. As a junior, he increased his already incredible totals to 44.2 and 1,148, and he won the scoring crown by an even wider margin. As a senior, his scoring figures of 44.5 and 1,381 were better yet, and no one even came close to challenging him for national honors.

The NCAA's college basketball all-time records book lists Maravich as the career scoring leader by almost 700 points more than the second-place scorer, Oscar Robertson. Maravich had a career scoring average of 44.2 (compared to Robertson's 33.8). Pete's more significant records include: season point total and average; career point total and average; most games scoring 50 or more points (both in a season [10] and in a career [28]); most field goals scored in a season (522) and a career (1,387); most free throws scored in a game (30) and in a three-year varsity tenure (893); and most field goals and free throws attempted in a season and a career.

Pete Maravich was to college basketball what Joe Namath was to pro football, what Willie Mays and Mickey Mantle had been to baseball, and what Gordie Howe has come to mean to hockey. He was invincible, incomparable, and, through it all, uncontrollable.

As ludicrous as it may seem, scoring is not the function Pete Maravich performs best. His gift (and it is a gift of great proportions) is ball-handling and dribbling, two parts of the game that he has refined and raised to the level of separate but equal art forms.

Ed Macauley, formerly a top pro performer with the Boston Celtics and the St. Louis Hawks and the Hawks' head coach for two seasons, offers the most appropriate comment on the way in which Maravich affects those seasoned observers who feel they have seen it all.

"Pete does things that make you say to yourself, 'Wait a minute, let me see you do that again.' It's like demanding an instant replay just so you can believe the incredible thing you've seen. Let me give you an example. I watched him pull off a stunt against Kentucky that made me shake my head, just as it would have made Red Auerbach or Red Holzman or Richie Guerin shake their heads. Pete came dribbling down the court right-handed, passed the ball between his legs, picked up the ball with his left hand, dribbled clear, and dropped in as pretty a lefthanded hook shot as you ever saw—from thirty feet.

"I haven't seen a ball-handler like him since Bob Cousy and Dick McGuire were in their prime. Pete can rip a team to shreds with his passes, just as Cousy and Mc-Guire could. But each of them had weaknesses as a shooter. Maravich has none. He can pop 'em in, long or short, right or left. There isn't a shot he can't make."

College coaches have their own views of Pete Maravich. Perhaps no one is more highly respected than Adolph Rupp, the head coach at Kentucky. After watching Maravich pump in five extremely long jump shots in as many attempts against the Wildcats, Adolph shook his head in grudging, frustrated admiration.

"If one of my boys had shot from that far out," said the Kentucky gentleman, "I would have had to jerk him out in a hurry. But there is no defense for anyone like him. He always finds a way to get the ball off, and to get it into that basket. I don't mind saying I was glad to see him graduate. We were able to go back to concentrating on how to stop *human* shooters."

Lou Carnesecca, who, as head coach of St. John's, had to deal with Maravich in a holiday tournament one season, said much the same things after Pete scored fifty-three points against the Redmen, forty of which he made in the second half.

"There are times when you say to yourself there's no way he has a shot. But he'll make a mid-air move, give you that double-pump action, and he will not only get the shot away, he'll make it." Carnesecca's experience with Maravich and LSU came in the Rainbow Classic in Honolulu, and the Hawaiians are still whispering about several fantastic plays Pete treated as routine.

The most electrifying pass he ever threw, they say, happened against St. John's in that Rainbow confrontation. Flashing downcourt on a fast break, Pete turned to look for the ball as he crossed the midcourt line. Turning, with the ball still behind him, he came face-to-face with a St. John's defender who had planted his feet and was openly inviting a charging violation. Just as suddenly, Maravich stopped, and with both hands reaching behind his back, he gathered in the ball. Then he whipped a bounce pass that zoomed through his legs and through the legs of the dumbfounded defender and carried thirty feet to teammate Bill Newton, all alone under the basket. The result was a ridiculously easy lay-up.

Later in the same game, as he was being forced out of bounds near midcourt, he threw a bullet pass behind his neck, sending the ball, chest-high, some twenty feet to Danny Hester, another unguarded teammate under the basket. Then, still later, he punched a pass in mid-dribble through six sets of clutching hands to Newton, again wide open underneath the hoop. It was, again, a sublimely easy shot for Newton.

But Hawaii was not the only scene of Maravich heroics. Indeed, every arena he has every played in has its own stories, and every fan who has witnessed him in action has a memory file of favorite moves and accomplishments to discuss.

They called Maravich a hot dog, a showboat, a grandstander. Many college coaches resented his rodeo-style basketball as well as the fact that his father, a member of their own select fraternity, tolerated such razzle-dazzle antics. But Press, who knew only too well the problems he would incur by taking his son with him to play at LSU, explains it this way:

"It was too good an opportunity to pass up. I never saw a kid able to do the things Pete did, and I didn't care if he was my son or the son of my most hated enemy. As a coach, I had to have him on my team. I had to work with that talent of his. It was as much an experience for me as it was for Pete, and we both learned many things about each other. I never let the fact that he was my son influence the attention he received on the court, or the amount of shots he took, or the favoritism he might have expected. My God, would Oscar Robertson's coach have had to be his father to give him the freedom he had? Would Bill Bradley's coach have done any more for him if he had been his father? It was a once-in-a-lifetime chance, and I was glad to take it.

"Sure, he went with me to LSU because I asked him, but he was as heavily recruited out of high school as any kid ever was, and he could have had his choice of any major school in the country. If I was selfish, so be it. But I like to think that, as a coach, 'recruiting' Pete enabled me to field a better team. I admit I had an edge, though," he adds with a twinkling smile.

One of the coaches who resented Maravich's tactics was Ray Mears, the head coach at the University of Tennessee, considered by many to have one of the finest defensive minds in the country. Neither man makes an attempt to cover up a dislike for the other. Some say it was

the result of a past feud, but many more insist that Mears'
ill feelings started when Pete Maravich began exploding
all his favorite defensive strategies.

In a game with LSU early in Pete's senior season, the
Maravich family did a job on Tennessee that should still
bring sparks to Mears' eyes if reminded of it. The result
of the game was a 71–59 conquest of the Tennessee Volunteers by LSU, but it was the way in which it was accomplished that rankled Mears.

With six minutes left, Press called a timeout. Pete came
to the sidelines, smiled at his father-coach, and said:
"Dad, let's put it in the deep freeze." Press nodded agree-
ment and could not completely restrain his mischievous
smile. He knew what was coming, but poor Ray Mears
did not.

The kids went back on the court, and the Tigers proceeded to play "stall-ball." Pete was the central figure. He
dribbled back and forth, in and out, weaving his way deli-
cately between frustrated and stymied Tennessee players.
He kept the fans in a state of boiling hysteria with a few
behind-the-back, crosscourt passes that hinted of sleight-
of-hand more than basketball skills. On the bench, Mears
fumed.

Pete made only twelve field goals in that game (he
took twenty-three shots), but one of them came near the
end of the six-minute freeze and was alone worth the
price of admission. It was a two-handed lay-up, thrown
back over his head at the basket, about ten feet away. He
had taken the shot blindly, not even looking for a fraction
of a second before releasing the ball, and with arrogant
confidence, he never looked back to see the ball rise in a
high arc and settle through the rim.

"You can't say I shot it blind," he insisted. "I knew
what I was doing. I knew where the basket was, and I
knew where the ball was going. I can do those kinds of

Lew Alcindor displays the shooting style that won the
NCAA basketball championship for UCLA in 1967. Left photo,
Alcindor (33) shoots over the head of Houston's
Elvin Hayes (44) in the semi-final game. Right photo, Lew
beats Dayton's Dan Sadlier (33) as he leads the Bruins to a
79–64 win in the finale.

Superstar Lew Alcindor was responsible for UCLA's domination of college basketball before he joined the Milwaukee Bucks as a professional.

Photo by Michael J. Flynn

AP Wirephoto

Calvin Murphy (23) jumps
in front of opposing
players to control loose ball
in a Niagara vs. LaSalle
College game.

Calvin Murphy, shooting,
had to outmaneuver and
outshoot taller players
throughout his college
career at Niagara.

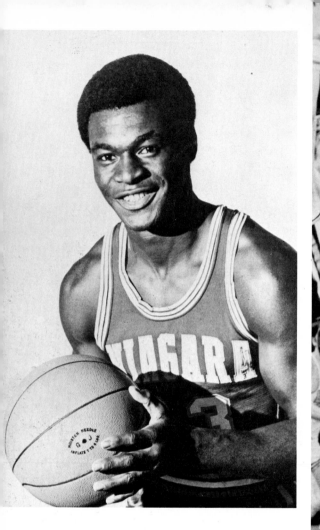

Calvin Murphy, Niagara's All-American
guard, now plays for the San Diego
Rockets of the NBA.

Left, Pistol Pete, dribbling, fakes Florida Gator Dan Boe as he drives in for a shot. Maravich now stars for the Atlanta Hawks.

Below, Pete Maravich, with ball, scored 69 points for LSU in this 1970 game against Alabama.

AP Wirephoto

Jo Jo White, dribbling, played college ball for Kansas; now he's a member of the Boston Celtics pro team.

Bob Lanier (31), formerly a St. Bonaventure College star, went on to play center for the Detroit Pistons.

Neal Walk, now with the Phoenix Suns, was a college luminary at the University of Florida.

Pete Maravich, Atlanta Hawks star, chats with youngsters at Campbell College basketball school, where Press Maravich, Pete's father, coaches during the summer.

Geoff Petrie, leaning toward ball, was a Princeton athlete before being drafted by the Portland Trail Blazers.

Bigman Dave Cowens (18) goes up for a shot. Dave played college ball for Florida State, now is a member of the Boston Celtics.

things. Don't ask me how, but I can do them. I'll make ten out of ten if I have to."

He could, and he would.

Peter Press Maravich was born in Sewickley, Pennsylvania, on June 22, 1948. He is the second son of Press Maravich, a basketball-playing Serbian from the coal mines of Aliquippa. Press is not his father's given name. "I was named Peter," says the father, "but in the kind of neighborhood I grew up in, Peter was a sissy name. So when I began to deliver newspapers—it was the *Pittsburgh Press*—I took that on as a nickname. When the guys began calling me Press instead of Peter, it sure sounded better.

"Then, when Pete was born, all my friends called him little Press. So we had no choice, really. We named him Peter Press Maravich."

Although born in Pennsylvania, Pete was the son of a vagabond basketball coach, and as such he learned to accept the uprooting of his home to keep pace with the changing locale of dad's jobs.

In 1950, Press took over as head coach at his alma mater, Davis-Elkins College in Elkins, West Virginia. But grammar school for little Pete was in Clemson, South Carolina, where Press had moved to become head coach at Clemson University.

Pete was a starter on the Daniel High School team while still in eighth grade, but the skinny little kid who used to challenge Clemson assistant coach Bobby Roberts to "shoot-outs" first began to make an impact as a scorer when he attended Edwards Military Academy in Salemburg, North Carolina. "One day I scored fifty points, and the next day the newspapers had it in big headlines," Pete recalls. "They just didn't seem to think it was possible for a prep school kid to score that much in one game. I think that kicked everything off. After that, folks got to be conscious of how many points I scored from game to game."

High school at Needham-Broughton resulted in a Prep All-America award and a deluge of college scouts. It was at this same time, too, that Press Maravich was offered a five-year, $15,000 per season contract to become head coach at LSU. "I always wanted to play for my dad," Pete says, "and I think, too, that he secretly wanted to coach me. We both knew how difficult it would be if we went to the same school, but the chance to revive basketball at a place like LSU was a challenge. Playing for my dad was a challenge sometimes too," he adds with a smile.

Thus it was done. LSU received two sets of autographs on the same day—one on a contract and one on a letter of intent—and those two signatures signaled the beginning of an incredible four years in the state of Louisiana.

LSU is, or was, a football school. The student body and the feverish fans in the state have always considered college football their prime attraction, and the Tigers, through the years, have always managed to bring top teams to the gridiron. LSU has had its share of football stars, several of whom have gone on to lasting fame in the professional ranks, notably Y. A. Tittle, Steve Van Buren, and Billy Cannon.

But basketball? "Not here," they said, "not at LSU." Basketball was merely a diversion, a distraction until the fall, something to help the populace get from the last Bowl game to the first spring practice. Bob Pettit, an NBA Hall of Fame member, was the only real superstar LSU basketball ever produced, although other such notable performers as Buddy Blair, Frank Brian, George Nattin, Joe Dean, Dick Maile, and Sparky Wade had worn the uniform of the Tigers. Their fame never extended much beyond the campus.

Now, however, basketball was about to go big-time at LSU. Pete Maravich had come to town, and he and his dad had to wait another season before they could capture the loyalty and imagination of college fans.

"We used to call them the Toothless Tigers," recalls Peter Finney, the associate sports editor of the New Orleans *States-Item.* "Basketball usually was a joke at LSU, after Pettit graduated. When the Maravich family hit town, the most the people would do was take a 'wait and see' attitude."

But they did not have long to wait, nor did they need much time to see just how sensational this 6'5" toothpick really was. He quickly became the talk of the school during his freshman season, and, according to Finney, this led to another source of embarrassment for the varsity.

"The crowds would pack the gym for the freshmen games that started at 5:45," he explains. "Then two hours later when the varsity tipped off, there was a traffic jam heading away from the Coliseum. Only a few thousand of the faithful would stay to see the Toothless Tigers, who won only three of twenty-six games that season."

The people were clearly entranced by the long-haired hero with the floppy socks, and he led the freshmen to a 16–1 record, losing the final game to Tennessee. He averaged 43.6 points per game and shot forty-five percent from the floor. Even that last-game defeat provided an insight into the competitive spirit of Pete Maravich. With eight seconds to play and LSU trailing by two points, Pete was fouled. He stepped to the line in a one-and-one situation. He made the first shot but missed the second, and the Baby Tigers were beaten by a point.

He was missing after the game, and there was cause for real concern until he turned up back at the hotel in Knoxville, having walked there alone from the fieldhouse, two miles away.

"I felt like I had let the team down," he said. "I just couldn't face any of them right after the game. I knew how badly they all wanted that undefeated season, and I had messed it all up by blowing a foul shot. A foul shot! The easiest thing in the world to make, and I had missed the biggest one I ever had to shoot."

But the freshman season, as important as it might have seemed to Pete Maravich at the time, was only the prelude to his career. Varsity basketball at LSU was about to enter the Age of Maravich, and no one knew it any better than Press, the coach and proud father of the budding star.

"Just wait until you see my boy," he told those who had, by some miracle, failed to see him as a freshman. "Just wait. You'll see something special."

Press never went into great detail about his offensive plans, nor did he feel the need to. Once, when pressured to make a statement about the shape of the team with Pete in the lineup, he managed to shed his restraint long enough to say: "I would have to be crazy not to let him shoot. He can do more things with the ball and without it than any other kid in the country. Cousy never saw such moves. Will he be this team's leading scorer? You bet your life he will, unless he breaks both legs. And if I know him, even that won't stop him. This kid lives for basketball. He'll play, and he'll shoot just as often as he can get clear. No doubt about it."

Pete's first taste of varsity competition was against the University of Tampa, no competition at all considering the volcano that erupted when Pete began shooting. He finished that first game with forty-eight points and took the national scoring lead, which for the next three years was never challenged. Among his more lofty totals in that first season were games of fifty-one points against Loyola of New Orleans; fifty-eight against Mississippi State; fifty-five against Auburn; fifty-two against state rival Tulane; fifty-two against Kentucky; fifty-four against Vanderbilt; and fifty-five against Tulane in the second meeting between the teams.

His low point total was seventeen against Tennessee's nationally famed defense. In the other meeting with Tennessee that season, Pete suffered through his second lowest output of the year, twenty-one points.

But his high-scoring game warrants description. LSU's Bob Pettit had established the Southeastern Conference single-game scoring record with fifty-eight points. In the Tigers' game with Alabama, with just seconds left to play, Pete had reached fifty-seven. LSU was in front by eight when teammate Ralph Jukkola recovered a loose ball. Instead of going back up with it for an easy lay-up, he passed all the way out to Maravich, who was standing almost near the midcourt line.

"He yelled at me to shoot," Pete recalls. "I didn't even know about the record, but apparently the other guys did. So I stepped toward the basket and let loose a silly two-handed push shot. Then I watched it go in."

Yes, he sank it, the incredible climax to an unforgettable game, and the crestfallen Alabama fans gave a standing ovation to this record-setter.

The post-season period after his sophomore year brought to Pete and Press one of the few disappointments they experienced during their three-year roller coaster ride to the top. The trials for the United States Olympic Team were being held and, naturally, Pete was invited to participate. He quickly accepted, and in the several games held between "teams" formed by the coaches, Maravich

became the fascinating, crowd-pleasing star. But the
team's coach, Oklahoma State's Hank Iba, decided
against Maravich's selection. Iba is a veteran coach, and
his theories and strategies are couched in the habits of the
old-timers. He searches for players who can play a disci-
plined, controlled offense and a stringent, obedient defense. Maravich did not fit this mold, nor did Rick Mount
of Purdue or Calvin Murphy of Niagara, the nation's
most exciting scorers. All three were left off the final
squad.

"Sure I felt bad about missing out on that," Pete ra-
tionalized, "but we could have won the Olympic basketball title with a bunch of cheerleaders."

And so he began to prepare for the junior season. Pete,
a worrier and a perfectionist, felt he had committed far
too many sophomore mistakes. He had led the nation in
scoring, he had been a unanimous All-America selection,
yet he was still not satisfied with his performance!

For one thing, he was disturbed with LSU's record, a
lukewarm 14–12. "If I was all that important to the
team," he said, "how come we didn't win a lot more? It
must have been something I was doing wrong.

"Well, for one thing, I forced too many shots," he explained. "I tried to score every time I thought I had a
shot, but there were lots of times I should have passed.
Yes, I remember each time. I have the ability—and
sometimes I don't think it's so good—to recall every play
of a game for a day or two after it is over. I lie awake and
remember all the mistakes and all the missed shots. I'm a
worrier. I'm never satisfied with my game, no matter how
many points I make."

Maravich also vowed to improve his rebounding and
his defense, although his rebounding was, by all normal
standards, superb. His defense was admittedly weak, but
Press insisted his son could make up for this deficiency

with his point totals. "Nobody can score with him," the father said, "so we have to come out ahead on any match-up."

Pete had collected 195 rebounds in his sophomore season, an average of better than seven per game. He had 105 assists, an average of four per game, which, if projected, resulted in 210 more points for LSU. But he was unhappy. "Until we have a winning season . . . no, until we have a championship season," he said, "I will not be doing my job for this team. I showed I could score a lot of points, but we didn't do much better than .500. Now we have to win and win big."

Although the scoring continued apace in his junior year (indeed, he scored more often), the record did not appreciably change. In fact, LSU slipped from 14–12 to 13–13.

Once again Maravich won the national scoring crown, with a 44.2 per game average fattened by such performances as fifty-two against Loyola, fifty-five against Tulane, fifty-three against Duquesne, fifty-two against Kentucky, fifty-eight against Georgia, fifty-five against Mississippi State, fifty-four against Auburn, fifty against Florida, and a staggering sixty-six in the second meeting of the season with Tulane.

His rebounding fell off slightly, to a total of 169 (or 6.5 per game), but his assists rose significantly, from the 105 as a sophomore to 126 as a junior, an average of five per game. This accounted for another 252 points for which he was indirectly responsible.

The early part of the junior season was a joy for the Maravich family and the rabid LSU supporters. The first eight games brought seven victories, and some of them were major accomplishments. A defeat of 5–0 Georgia preceded LSU's drive to the championship of the All-College Tournament in Oklahoma City, in which LSU beat

Wyoming (with a record of 8–0 at the time), Oklahoma City University, and a 9–0 Duquesne team for the title. Pete averaged forty-six points per game, shooting almost fifty percent in the three pressure-packed contests, and he had LSU sailing well above what its true level of quality was destined to be that season.

Sure enough, five straight setbacks brought the Tigers to a 7–6 mark. From that point on, the remaining games of the season were spent trying to rise above .500, an accomplishment that was not realized.

"There were still things to be done, parts of my game to improve," Pete said at the conclusion of the season. "But most important is to win a championship for the team. My dad has worked a long time, and he never has had a real championship team, and we have the necessary talent to get him one. That will be our goal in the senior year."

Individually, however, the junior season of 1968–1969 was an artistic success for young Pete Maravich. He had increased his shooting percentage from forty-two to forty-four percent, he had increased his assist totals, and he had scored more points in fewer shots (976, as compared to 1,022 as a sophomore). He had proved invincible to every type of defense except the one employed by Tennessee, the team that was to prove his nemesis throughout his college career. (As a junior, his two low-scoring games, of twenty-one and twenty points, were again against the Volunteers. Each time he made just eight of eighteen field goal tries.)

Against Loyola and Pittsburgh, he made eleven assists, and he engineered ten assists against Mississippi State. Not once in the sophomore season had he reached double figures in assists, and while he registered zero assists in two games as a sophomore, that did not happen in his junior year.

The senior season almost turned out as it should have for Pete and Press. Although LSU did not win the SEC championship, the conference for the first time lifted its ban on teams accepting only NCAA tournament's invitations, and the National Invitation Tournament in New York quickly tendered an offer to the Tigers from Bayou country. It was quickly accepted by Press, Pete, and the rest of the team, and not just for the opportunity to see New York.

"A championship is a championship," Pete said, "and if we win the NIT, it will be good enough. I thought we had enough to beat Kentucky in the SEC and qualify for the NCAA tournament, but it didn't work out. Now we have been given another chance, and I'm as excited as I have ever been. Bring 'em on."

There are those who suggested that New York City is the natural habitat for a showman such as Pete Maravich. "If that kid could have gone to a school in New York," suggested Lou Carnesecca, "he would have had headlines in every paper every day. Heck, he might have had his own television show. It will be nice to see him in the NIT . . . nice, that is, except for the teams who have to play LSU. The kid will shoot their eyes out to win this tournament."

The locale was Madison Square Garden, a shining new tribute to glass and steel. LSU's first game was against a solid team from Georgetown. The NIT committee had decreed that it would be televised nationally so it was played on a Sunday afternoon. The fans—and there was a sellout total of 19,500 of them—were there to watch this young Houdini do his magical thing. While he did not let them down, he did not shatter any scoring records either.

Georgetown covered him well, using a sticky triangle-and-two defense conceived by coach Jack Magee. In a triangle-and-two, three men are assigned duties intended

to stop a superscorer. In this case, Mike Laska stuck with
Maravich, Don Weber chased the ball, and a third man
chased Pete. Maravich scored twenty, making only six of
sixteen field goal attempts, but he had five assists and six
rebounds. Teammate Danny Hester picked up the slack
by scoring thirty points on a 12-for-21 performance. LSU
won 83–82.

Apple Sanders, 6'7", pulled in seventeen rebounds.
Billy Newton had ten and Hester, eight. The other guard,
Jeff Tribbett, did what was expected of him—he passed
off to Maravich. As an interesting aside, it should be no-
ted that Tribett had been well-prepared for this line of
work since his schoolboy days, for he had attended high
school in Indiana with Rick Mount, and there, too, he
was the "other" guard. "I'm used to passing off to star
shooters," he cracked. "I just wouldn't feel right taking
more than a few shots." He had taken six against Georgetown and missed them all.

The Tigers moved to the quarterfinal round, when they
took on the quick Oklahoma team led by the high-scoring
Garfield Heard, a powerful 6'6" forward. Again it was
close, but again LSU made it through. Maravich registered thirty-seven points, the tournament high. He made
fourteen of thirty-three field goal attempts, had nine assists, and recovered eight rebounds. Hester added twenty
points, and Sanders pulled down nineteen rebounds. LSU
won 97–94.

The excitement was building, for the next opponent in
the semifinal round was Marquette, a vastly talented team
coached by Al McGuire and paced by the brilliant All-
America guard, 6'3" Dean Meminger, another product of
the New York street playgrounds in Harlem.

McGuire had established the reputation of being a
maverick. He had been offered a coaching job two years
previously by the newly formed Milwaukee Bucks of the

NBA, and he had agreed to accept it. But Marquette's administration, reluctant to lose such a prized coach, refused to let him terminate a contract that still had several years to run. McGuire's disappointment was only momentary. "If I have to stay here," he said wistfully, "I couldn't be much better off. I'll have Meminger (then about to become a sophomore), and if I am going to remain at Marquette, I promise that, with this kid, we will bring a national championship to the school."

In the 1969–1970 season, Marquette had lost just three of twenty-three games and emerged as the fifth-ranked team in the country. Marquette entered the NIT after becoming one of the few teams in history to turn down an NCAA at-large invitation. Why?

"They wanted us to play our regional games in Texas," McGuire fumed. "We are from the midwest. What would we be doing in some small town in Texas? The NCAA wouldn't change its mind, and so I wouldn't change mine either. I told them thanks, but no thanks. We sort of expected, once that happened, to hear from the NIT people."

McGuire, a native New Yorker, a star for St. John's University, and a defensive stickout for the Knicks, knew very well that the NIT would call, and he knew that the NIT would be more than delighted to have the nation's fifth-ranked team in its field.

McGuire's decision was a wise one, for the Warriors went through four NIT games almost untouched and, indeed, took back a national championship to the Milwaukee campus of Marquette. The third victim of the Marquette steamroller was LSU. The score was 101–79.

It was a game in which all the odds were stacked against Pistol Pete. He was covered by Meminger, a unanimous All-America that year. If Maravich missed, Ric Cobb, Joe Thomas, and Gary Brell rescued the plays

with defensive rebounds. Thomas, at 6'6" had fourteen rebounds and twenty-eight points. Cobb, 6'5", scored twenty points, missing only one of ten field goal tries. Meminger had sixteen points and five assists.

But Pete wowed the crowd with his fancy passing and
ball-handling, and the New York basketball fans, the
most appreciative in the country in their admiration of the
finer points of the game, went wild with delight. Pete in-
cited several bursts of spontaneous applause and a few
hysterical cheers, and several times overenthusiastic fans
ran out onto the court to try to shake his hand.

Maravich scored only twenty points, a dismal 4-for-13
from the floor. However, he had nine assists. Meminger,
for one, was not very much impressed. "I've seen all
those tricks," he said, "and I'm not so sure they belong on
a college basketball team. I've seen fancier players than
Maravich in the Harlem playgrounds, but that's too much
of an individual game for college. But I must admit he is
pretty good at what he does."

Maravich was bitterly disappointed. "I was lousy," he
said. "We should have run more. We should have won.
Those other guys played their hearts out, and I let them
down. I let my dad down, too. I was lousy."

He was not, however, without honor in the NIT. He
was named to the tournament's prestigious All-Star team,
and his three-game totals of seventy-seven points, twenty-three assists, and fifteen rebounds were more than
commendable. He was a sensation.

But his college career had ended, and no championship
had accrued to LSU. "We gave our best," a disappointed
Press Maravich said. "All of them played hard, including
Pete. Sure, I'm sorry we didn't win this tournament, but it
was an honor to be invited and to play in New York, and
there certainly is no disgrace in losing to a team like Marquette. That's as good a team as I've ever seen. Al has

done an outstanding job with them, and I'm not so sure he couldn't have won the NCAA if he had chosen to enter it. But I understood his reasons, and I, for one, agree with him. But if he had gone to the NCAA," Press grinned, "we might have won the NIT."

The weeks and months of turmoil and indecision began. Maravich, always an intense young man who held basketball above all else, was a study in mental fatigue. The almost unyielding pressure had come to a halt, but the strain had immediately picked up again in other areas. He no longer experienced the tension associated with playing, for his collegiate playing was done, but he suffered the tension resulting from the professionals' pursuit.

Pete had never been calm or placid. He had admitted that he could not sleep the night before and the night after a game. He admitted to being "up-tight" about the added stress of playing for his father, of trying to explain to fans and reporters that he did not receive any special treatment because of their relationship.

His conflicts with officials were frequent and deplorable. Several times he had fouled out, and a few times his outbursts of temper had even resulted in jangled nerves that interfered with his performance. Press, whose temper matched his son's, was also penalized several technical fouls as a result of behavior not in the best interests of competition.

In February of 1969, in an SEC match with Vanderbilt, LSU was trailing by a scant three points with less than two minutes to play when Maravich insisted he had been fouled. The officials did not agree, and when no whistle was blown and no free throws awarded, Pete exploded. He fumed and raved and uttered several tactless epithets. He was consequently ejected from the game. LSU went on to lose 85–83.

There were other such displays of temper and other

ejections from equally crucial games, and to some people Pete had become the epitome of a spoiled brat. But it was his intense competitive nature that caused such acts of frustration, and most people tried at least to understand the motivation for his behavior.

"Pete has tremendous talent," an SEC official said, "but he would greatly benefit from a good kick in the rear."

Another referee told a New Orleans newspaper reporter that "if he doesn't control his temper, he is going to alienate the officials, and they'll look for the calls that go against him. He invites such things."

Tantrums notwithstanding, both the NBA and the ABA were anxious to obtain the services of this long-haired magician. The bidding never opened low. The ABA, through its Carolina Cougars, offered a package of $1.9 million. The NBA, although not sure yet which of its teams would ultimately draft him, matched that figure.

Several unconfirmed rumors stated that the ABA offered a contract twice—one of $1.9 million to Pete and one of $50,000 per year for life to Press. Another report came out of Pittsburgh, insisting that the father-son duo was headed there, to play and coach for that faltering franchise. All along, however, both Maraviches steadfastly denied such stories. "We heard a lot about those deals in the papers," Press said. "After Pete graduates, you know, he would go to a team and I would be named its coach. What a lot of bunk. Sure, I might take a pro coaching job. What if I get offered $50,000 for life? What am I supposed to do, turn it down? But right now Pete's future and mine are two different things."

The choice, then, was Pete's to make. "Pete wanted to make his own decision," Press said. "I can't blame him. We knew he would be able to play in either league, and so other things entered into his thinking. Not money, and not getting a quick chance to play. Other things."

Chief among those other considerations was, it is said, location. Pete had never lost his affection for the deep south, the area in which he grew up and attended grammar school and high school. That seemed to put the Cougars on top. It was an ABA franchise operating on a statewide level of appeal, and it used three cities in North Carolina—Charlotte, Greensboro, and Raleigh—as its home sites. The assumption stood up when the NBA's order of draft was announced. Detroit had been awarded the first selection, San Diego, the second, and San Francisco, the third. Pete had never considered the idea of playing in California, and the Pistons made no attempt to hide their desire for St. Bonaventure's hulking center, Bob Lanier. But the NBA was determined to find a home for Maravich within its structure, so a deal was arranged in which San Francisco traded its choice to Atlanta for the right to negotiate with Zelmo Beatty, a former Hawk center who had jumped his contract to join the ABA. Suddenly, to the chagrin of the ABA, another southern city was in the picture, and it was Maravich's sense of competition that entered his thinking when he issued his next, and final, announcement.

"Atlanta is fine," he said. "I wanted to go back to the south, and that's where Atlanta is. Now I can choose between Carolina and Atlanta, and there isn't really that much of a distance difference. But there is a competition difference. I have to play with the best to see what I can do. If I choose the ABA, I know I'll start right away. But if I choose the NBA and manage to start, I will have proved something to myself. I am very happy with this arrangement, and I believe I will sign with the Hawks."

And so, as had happened a year earlier with Lew Alcindor, the NBA gathered in the country's top player of the year. The San Diego Rockets, well aware of what had transpired, passed Maravich in their first selection and drafted Rudy Tomjanovich, a 6'8" forward from Michigan. Then Atlanta, drafting in San Francisco's stead, chose Peter Press Maravich.

Carolina, desperate in its own needs and commitments, nevertheless drafted Pete in the first five rounds, hoping that he would change his mind. The ABA does not, or at least in those days did not, release its rounds one by one. Five at a time are announced, and no team lists the players in the order in which they were drafted.

Negotiations with the Hawks proceeded smoothly. The talking went slowly, but not because Pete was holding out or considering the ABA and not because he was trying to use the ABA as a wedge to increase the Atlanta offer. "We had agreed on the money," he said, "but we were trying to set it up so that I could best handle the tax end of it. It was a complicated contract, with lots of deferred payments."

Finally, the formal signing took place, but new troubles were in store for the Hawks.

In this day, the mention of such difficulty is sad and demeaning; nonetheless, the racial issue was introduced. Under the personable and capable Richie Guerin, the young coach of the team, the Hawks had gone to the Western Conference playoff finals before losing to the Lakers the year before. There they had set up that memorable New York–Los Angeles seven-game championship series. But Atlanta was a solid team, offensively brilliant and led by several outstanding players to whom losing was a serious affront.

Those players were black; guards Lou Hudson and Walt Hazzard, forwards Joe Caldwell and Bill Bridges, and center Walt Bellamy. They had, for the most part, been responsible for engineering the Hawks' 48–34 record, which had been good enough to win the Western Conference's regular season championship.

The questions that arose now were these:

Would Guerin break up a near-championship team in order to include a rookie with a $1.9 million price tag?

Would Maravich, with a southern background and prior experience in a "lily white" athletic atmosphere, be accepted by the black players who knew that however talented Maravich was, he was not yet ready to step in and do the job as a functioning, complete professional?

Would the resentment caused by his exorbitant contractual terms and the benching of one of the regulars cause a rift on the team?

Clearly, Guerin was on the spot. He wanted to win, naturally, and he wanted to win with the best players he could field. But the fans had cheered the acquisition of Maravich, and they would demand to see him in action. He was a ready-made—and white—hero. While coaches do not necessarily concern themselves with the feelings and wishes of such fans, they do react strongly to the threat of faltering attendance and widespread disenchantment.

"The five best players will start," Guerin decided. "I don't care who they are or what color they are or where they come from. If they can help this team, they'll play. We know Pete has great talent. We also know that he is a rookie and that he has much to learn about the pro game. If he proves good enough to handle it, he'll play. Until he does learn enough, he'll sit. Period."

The most frequent form of criticism of Maravich's style heard during that summer training camp period was of his individuality, both on and off the court. In the pros, basketball is a team sport. No one takes shots that are not good percentage shots. No one goes out of his way to execute a fancy pass that might go astray when a sure-hand-ed, unspectacular one will do the job.

No one, with the possible exception of an Alcindor or a Jerry West, could expect a team to be arranged around his abilities, as was the case with Pete at LSU.

At first, the other Hawks were annoyed with the pub-licity and the attention Pete received. They were, no doubt, envious also of the money he received, but what infuriated them most was the thought that he might be moved into a starting role before he was ready, simply to justify his millionaire's contract.

To their credit, they rarely spoke out about the situa-tion. They kept it to themselves, and while Maravich did not become their instant friend, he did earn their grudging respect as a player.

Meanwhile, one of the problems eliminated itself. Mo-tivated either by money, by the chance to become an even greater star, or by the presence of Pete, Joe Caldwell jumped to the ABA early in the season; coincidentally, he went to the same Carolina Cougars who had been so bit-terly disappointed when they lost Maravich.

This accomplished one thing: it opened a spot on the starting team. Hudson was asked by Guerin to move to forward, and the All-Star guard graciously agreed. Mar-avich teamed with Hazzard in the backcourt, and the more he played, the faster he developed. He became a high scorer, but, more significantly, he became a passing whiz, a collector of assists, and a true team player.

As Pete continued to see steady action, the players warmed to him. As he proved he could convert his talents to a pro game, his teammates began to appreciate what he would mean to the team in achieving its ultimate goal, winning.

"I know," he said early in the rookie season, "that my ball-handling can be much better than it's been. But these things are going to smooth themselves out. It's just like anything else where you're working with new people. It takes time to adjust to different players. For three seasons at LSU, I did nearly all the shooting, the dribbling, and the passing. I handled the ball seventy-five percent of the time. Not now, though. Now it's more like ninety percent of the time that I don't have the ball."

However, he added, his adjustment from passer and ball-handler to "receiver" has not been overly difficult.

"We have a great ball-handler here—Walt Hazzard. When he has the ball, I've learned to do one thing . . . get the heck out of his way. I know he'll get the ball to me if I'm clear."

When Pete does have the ball, he has started to think more in terms of assists than baskets. "I know everybody on this team can score," he said. "I wouldn't begin to think I am a better shooter than Lou Hudson, for instance. He's just fantastic. I am trying to do what is necessary to win, and that means being a team player. Picking up assists, making the passes that lead to easy baskets —that's what I have come to look for. I pride myself on getting the ball to the guys who score. If I do that, I'm doing my job. I played thirty-two minutes one night and took only thirteen shots. That's a far cry from the thirty-five and forty shots a game I used to take in college. But I don't care about that. I don't let that bother me. This is pro basketball, the highest level of the game there is. It's a job and a business. There's no sense of individualism any more because all the players are so danged good."

But the showman in him sneaks through on occasion. "I had eight assists in Cleveland," he smiles, "on eight different kinds of passes, including a fifty-foot rolling pass that got to Lou on one bounce. I'm learning how to react with these players, and when I can suit my game to theirs, I'll be that much more valuable."

Pete still bristles when he is reminded of all the people who said he has no sense of team discipline, no respect for the other players on the team. "That's a lot of baloney," he says. "There are always fifty percent of the people who like and fifty percent who don't, in anything you do. That's the way this world lives. There are people who were disgusted with me, who said I'd never be able to play in the NBA. I'd rather worry about a gnat than about those people."

Another interesting development once Maravich began playing regularly was the amount and type of praise heaped on him by opposing players and coaches. Walt Frazier of the Knicks, for instance, has seen a difference between the college Maravich, the rookie Maravich, and the Maravich of today.

"He has developed a lot of confidence in his shooting since we played Atlanta in a pre-season game," Frazier said after Pete had scored forty points against the Knicks in New York. "His passing is so much better, too. He has shortened up on his dribble, and he controls it better. He doesn't push it out in front as much as he used to. He has long arms and is quick and deceptive."

Slowly, surely, Maravich began to climb in the NBA's scoring standings. He had moved his average up to more than twenty points per game by mid-season of his rookie year, and his assists had reached the average he maintained at LSU, better than five per game. He was showing also some strength as a rebounder, while holding down the second scoring spot on the team, behind Hudson, an All-Star who had many more minutes of game time and had taken many more shots.

Now Guerin can speak more definitively about his budding superstar. Now he can reflect on what impact Maravich might have on the Hawks in the years to come, and he predicts a bright, glowing future.

"Great natural ability," Guerin begins. "Fantastic feel for the game. He has come a long way in a very short period of time, and that indicates to me that he will become far better. He is the ideal height for a guard in today's game. He is a good jumper and, regardless of the way he might appear physically, he is strong enough for this game. He can take the punishment, and he can dish some out too. As a passer, I don't think I've seen many better in my years with the pros [which began in 1956 when Guerin joined the Knicks as a rookie from Iona College in New York City and embarked on a fourteen-year pro career].

"I think he'll become a superstar in this league. The kid is all basketball. He thinks about it every minute. He's always working, always practicing, trying to get the mistakes out of his game. He had a great deal of pressure on him when he signed as a rookie, and when he began to play, everybody wanted a chance to shoot him down. But he has become consistent, despite the pressure, and that is the mark of a good pro."

Not a man to mince words, Guerin spoke out on the early season difficulties encountered by Maravich and, as a result, by himself. "He had pressure applied unfairly," Richie said. "It took a while until the players adjusted to him, and took the same time span for him to adjust to them. But I don't think there ever was much strain of a racial nature. I suppose some of the players resented him because of the publicity and the attention. They had to get to know him. Now they do, and I don't think anyone on this team thinks anything but good thoughts about Pete Maravich."

The other problem, an indirect result of Maravich's presence, was the stunning loss of Caldwell. "Pete had to make the rest of the team see he could take Joe's place," is how Guerin puts it. "That just added to the pressures already present, but he came through. After the initial readjustment period without Caldwell, we started playing good basketball. I like to play a run-and-shoot kind of offense. It can be very effective when you have the right personnel. Look at how far the fast break took those great Celtic teams. Pete is ideally suited to such a game, and we feel he'll continue to improve."

Other coaches talk about the star status of Maravich and the star treatment they insist he has begun to receive from officials. In one game in New York, a member of the Knicks brushed lightly past Pete, who had the ball—a dubious violation at best—but two whistles sounded immediately.

Red Holzman, New York's coach, leaped off the bench in a rage. "He's not a superstar yet," Red snarled at the nearest official. "He's just a kid."

Yet there is no doubt Maravich has an attraction about him that captivates even the referees. Jack Rohan, the coach at Columbia, can remember one other player who had the same effect—Bill Bradley, when he was an All-America at Princeton. "A kid like Bradley used to hypnotize the officials," Rohan said. "Most of them, anyway. There are always a few who are determined to 'show up that hotshot.' That's the other extreme, and neither are particularly equitable. But kids with that kind of Bradley charisma do have that effect on people."

Babe McCarthy, who was the head coach of the New Orleans Buccaneers (now the Memphis Pros) of the ABA, saw a lot of Pete in college and has seen much of him since. "He is the most exciting player in the United States," McCarthy said. "He isn't afraid to try anything. You'll have some players who practice all those unorthodox moves, but when you put them into a game, they'll never use them. Not Maravich. He improvises to meet the circumstances. There's no question in my mind that he is the most exciting player in the country today. What I'm saying is he's far more of a crowd-pleaser than someone like Lew Alcindor, although I don't want to take anything away from Lew. Pete's the master of the unexpected, and that's what makes people remember him and talk about him."

Although Maravich was only twenty-three years old as a rookie, he had matured far beyond that age in basketball skill.

He has always, it seems, been involved in sensational efforts. During his days in grammar school and high school, he was building his talents, preparing them for college basketball. "I remember, as a kid, I always had my basketball with me," he says. "I'd bounce it home from school and in the house. I even took it to the movies on Saturdays and made sure I sat in an aisle seat so I could bounce it during the show. Basketball has always been part of me, the biggest, most important part. Sometimes it interferes with basic things like sleeping and eating. I never could sleep after a game. I'd go over every play, trying to see what I could have done that would have been better or maybe how the team could have played better. Some guys can play a game and forget it and think only about the next one. Not me. I can't forget a game, whether we win or lose, but particularly when we lose. I know there are things I can do better, and thinking about it keeps me all wound up."

Perhaps his attraction to the game is too deep, for Pete has been accused of being unsympathetic to players during a game and to interviewers after a game. But his affinity to basketball is so deeply rooted that it takes precedence over all other things.

Most annoying to Maravich, and likewise to other star athletes, are the questions of reporters. They are always repeating the same questions, regardless of how many times they have been asked before. "Like when I was in college," he says, "I guess I was asked a thousand times what it was like to play with my father as the coach, and I answered it a thousand times. I felt like a wind-up doll. 'No, there isn't any friction because my dad coaches the team . . . He's the coach and he runs the team . . . Yes, I do like playing for my dad . . . no, I wouldn't do it any differently if I had it to do all over again.' But it seems people never stop asking that one, even now.

"Now in the pros there are other pat questions, and I don't see any other alternative but to give pat answers. I mean, if I kept changing my answers just to try for a little variety, people would feel I was insincere. They ask me if I have had much trouble adjusting to the pro game . . . if I get along with my teammates . . . if I miss shooting as often as I used to. They ask about my private life, but some parts of my life are my own and I won't talk about them.

"Sure, I have a girl friend. I've always dated, but I like to keep that part of it to myself. There are guys who like to be seen with girls and to talk about them. That's their business. I just don't like to talk about my private life."

It has been a long time since Pete Maravich was introduced to this complicated game that would rule his life. He was six years old in Clemson, South Carolina, as the story goes, when his dad bought him a basketball for Christmas. But he ignored the strange round object.

One day he was in the backyard watching his dad shoot a few (yes, there was a backboard close by—Press saw to that). Press made a few. Pete, always cocky, figured it was easy and said that he'd like to try. He took a shot and missed, and Press recalls now "when I saw him get angry, I knew I had him hooked."

Hooked indeed. "There were years when I was a kid," Pete says, "when I bet I played ball forty-seven weeks out of the year and eight to ten hours a day during the summer months."

Press, a basketball addict long before Pete ever heard the sweet sound of the bounce and swish, made sure he kept his son's interest alive. "He used to need money, you know, for candy and movies and like that," the father remembers, "but I made him make his quota of baskets before I gave him any. I had no idea how good he was going to be, but I knew I wanted him to play. Basketball has always been good to me, and anything that much fun couldn't be bad for my son."

Perhaps one of the necessary ingredients to Pete's success is his cockiness. He is convinced about his talent. "I once saw a pro game on television when I was in high school," he says, "and I remember watching Hal Greer [a twenty thousand-plus point scorer in the NBA]. I said to myself 'boy, I'd like to go a little one-on-one against him.' And I meant it."

Coaches have described Maravich as "a blend of Cousy and Oscar, with a little more hot dog thrown in." Others have called him "Houdini in short pants" and still others, less impressed by his style, have used such words as "selfish" and "gunner" in describing his performance.

But he survived the first few critical months with the Hawks, and his future is wide open now. Bill Bridges, Atlanta's star forward, tells it.

"He was very much withdrawn," says the articulate graduate of Kansas University. "He'd hold his arms crossed against his chest when he sat on the bench, and in the airports he'd always be by himself. We are a team. We are not individuals. Personally, I was not willing to accept him as a teammate. We have relaxed our resistance now and we accept him as an individual. In the dressing room now he's started to smile and relax. In the airports he has opened up. He has begun to come to us and chat. We got together twice trying to establish what was wrong when we were losing early in his rookie season. We had to disclose our own feelings. I don't think we were fighting each other. I don't think we were divided as a team, but there was some conflict. Mainly it was the rest of us, embarrassed that we weren't putting it together. Pete has the potential of being a great pro, but he can't control the ball all the time. He'll get better, and we'll be winners with him."

Pete's charisma attracts others with the same magnetism, just as Joe Namath acts as a lure for show business personalities. Al Hirt, the rotund trumpeter who has made New Orleans a way of life in the lore of American jazz, has long been a Maravich worshipper.

"Y'all gonna love Pete Maravich," he drawls. "Listen heah. Pete is gonna become the Babe Ruth of pro basketball. He's gonna become what Joe Namath is to pro football. Y'all ain't gonna have enough seats in Atlanta when he starts a-playin' for them Hawks. He's gonna miss some shots, but he's still gonna be fantastic. I took Hank Stram [head coach of pro football's Kansas City Chiefs] to see him, and he just didn't believe it. He said, 'Man, what a flanker he'd make!' Can you believe that? I truly believe he's the greatest athlete around."

Pete's dramatic rise to stardom as a rookie came about in mid-November of 1970, when Guerin took him from the bench and put him into the starting lineup. In the next six games—the first half dozen he had ever started—his point totals were twenty-three, twenty-eight, thirty-two, thrity-two, thirty-two and forty. "Guerin patted me on the rear a few times after I came out of some of those games," Pete remembers, "and that was when I came over the hill from disgust."

Now the best players praise him, such as Frazier of the Knicks. "He makes some unbelievable shots," says Walt. "He double-pumps a couple of times, and then he banks it in. What can you do? He's shooting deeper and deeper, and they are not easy shots."

Red Holzman, too, finds awe. "He makes things up in midair, taking all kinds of shots. He changes the tempo of a defense. We can set up fast enough to provide help on him, but it makes us change from what we like to do."

Pete intends to make the most of his career. "Playing in the pros," he says, "with these great individuals, is the top of any totem pole. It's more fun than college ball because it's so great to play with these guys. It'll be even easier for me eventually. No, I haven't given up my show-time stuff. I just haven't used it yet."

Pete has survived. He has survived the pressure of playing for his father under a spotlight that only national exposure can create. He has survived the stigma of his million-dollar contract. He has survived the dissension on his team that his presence caused. He has made it as a starter and a star in the finest basketball league in the world.

Those who witnessed his rookie season were awed at the rapidity of his progress and convinced that he was a superstar in the making. His coach, other coaches, his teammates, opponents, and his fans speak in glowing terms of this whippet-thin guard with the mod hair, the floppy socks (one pair of which has been given to the Basketball Hall of Fame) and the soulful brown eyes.

Indeed, the best part of basketball, for Pete, may be ahead of him. But even if he did not play another minute, what he has accomplished already would be an inspiration to all basketball players and fans.

"I have no doubt that I will make it," he says. "Soon, I

can feel it, one of these nights it's all going to work. I just know it's coming."

Pete Maravich is only 6'5". But in terms of the promise of what he may one day do in this game, no one stands any taller.

4

Five for the Money

IT is the unanimous opinion of knowledgeable basketball observers across the county that Lew Alcindor, Calvin Murphy, and Pete Maravich are cut from superstar cloth. No one can doubt the accuracy of such predictions when measured against their accomplishments to date.

Yet these experts have expressed the thought that five other young men will join The Big Three in their throne room. There is evidence that these five, two of whom were rookies in the 1969–1970 season and the other three in the 1970–1971 campaign, are bound to appear on All-Star teams frequently during the next ten years.

They are Neal Walk of the Phoenix Suns, Geoff Petrie of the Portland Trail Blazers, Bob Lanier of the Detroit Pistons, and Dave Cowens and Jo Jo White of the Boston Celtics.

Walk, Lanier, and Cowens are centers, the vital players

around whom their teams have begun to operate. These young men hold down the position that must be played with superb competence if any team is to find success.

Petrie and White are guards, the top examples of the new breed of guard that has appeared as a result of the evolution of the game itself. In addition to the normal demands of dribbling, passing, and ball-handling, these two have become adept at shooting, defense, and rebounding. They are, along with Murphy and Maravich, the most impressive young guards in the NBA.

These five have likewise had to overcome their share of obstacles. They have met with injury and rejection. They have been overly praised or wrongly ignored, but their achievements have been, as a result, all the more rewarding. In any book entitled *Rookie: The World of the NBA,* their efforts must be recognized.

These five have become steady, dependable, and valuable additions to their teams. They have not broken down under pressure; rather, they have matured and developed when faced with the pressure associated with performing in the NBA. They are truly complete professionals.

They are Five for the Money.

This comment about Neal Eugene Walk serves to sum up the man: "He tries about as hard as anyone I've seen," says head coach Cotton Fitzsimmons of the Phoenix Suns. "He's big and strong and well-schooled in basketball. But it's his desire that is most impressive. I've never known anyone so intense, so determined to make it."

This, then, is what Neal Walk is all about. He is a 6'10", 250-pound center who was, rather surprisingly, drafted on the first round by the Suns, the second player in the country to be claimed in the NBA's 1969 draft meeting. Lew Alcindor was the only player to be drafted ahead of him.

"Everyone knew Alcindor was going to be the first draft choice," explains Jerry Colangelo, the general manager and former interim head coach of the team. "Everyone knew we had that coin flip with the Milwaukee Bucks to see which of us was going to get to make that selection. Well, we lost. Everyone knows that, too. The Bucks took Alcindor. Then we drafted Neal, and it seems a lot of people found that surprising. I don't know why. We needed a center. We had him as the second-best center in the country on all our scouting reports that year. I think Milwaukee might have taken him if we had won that coin toss."

There was, however, good reason for surprise. It was felt at the time that, although Walk was the second best center available, he did not even approach Alcindor in potential or talent. Most experts predicted that the Suns would choose a forward or a guard, since high grade players at both positions were available. It was felt that Phoenix would defer the drafting of a center until the following season, when Lanier, among others, would be eligible. Besides, the Suns did have 6'10" Jim Fox, a more than adequate center who would have been able to hold down the position for another season.

But they chose Neal Walk of the University of Florida.

"Was I surprised? Well, a little, I suppose," says Walk, a supremely confident athlete. "I don't think anyone expected Alcindor to be picked anywhere else but first. I can see, though, why they might have been surprised that I went next. But I wasn't that shocked. I knew I would go on the first round. I knew Phoenix was in need of a center. I sort of expected what happened. I was flattered but not dumbfounded. Just pleased and flattered, I guess."

The native of Brooklyn, New York, who moved to Miami, Florida, when his father joined an advertising organization there, spoke candidly about his prospects and potential soon after he discovered he was to become one of the Phoenix Suns.

"I'm going to like playing in Phoenix," he said, "and not just for the great weather. The advantage of going to an expansion team like the Suns is that you learn with them. And I'll get a chance to play regularly, I hope. If I was drafted by a team with a great center, or just a generally super team, I imagine I would get a lot less court time. This has to make me happy, because I want to play. I think I can develop faster and improve more quickly with a young team, and we have the chance to mature together as players, to experience a real unity. Not many rookies get the same advantages, as I see it."

Neal's reasoning is sound, and the points he made were logical. But much remained for him to prove. Most importantly, he would have to give sufficient evidence that he could, indeed, compete successfully in the towering world of the NBA centers.

"I know it might have been easier for me if I had chosen to play in the ABA," he says, "and I did consider it. I had a few very attractive offers. But I felt this way about it. I wanted to see if I could play with the best. Every athlete wants to find that out, like it's a matter of great personal pride. I looked forward to working with the Suns, and their coach at the time, John Kerr, was a former All-Star NBA center. I had a lot to learn, and I figured this was a man I could learn from. I could have played in the ABA, but I wanted to play in the NBA."

Walk's style of basketball is similar to that of the New York City playground athlete. Yet he owes no special allegiance to New York and, in fact, he earned his three varsity letters at Miami Beach Senior High School.

But he has remained a center in the mold of the "old

school" of basketball. He establishes a strong position about midway between the baseline and the free throw line, on either side of the twelve-foot lane. He is then in position to execute several maneuvers: taking a pass while using his body to protect both the ball and his area; turning for a jump shot; making that first critical step toward the launching of a drive to the basket; fading back for a one-handed push shot; cutting across the lane for a hook shot; feeding off to teammates sliding past him— the "give-and-go" play; and enabling himself to remain in a good position for offensive rebounding.

On defense, Walk has learned to use his reach, not his body, the most difficult lesson to be learned by overly large and not exceptionally agile centers. He is a defensive rebounder of terrifying strength, crashing the boards with the full impact his 250 pounds can supply and standing up well under the physical beating all inside men in the NBA must take.

Defense had not always been Walk's forte, especially after he entered the NBA. It is a tribute to his determination that he has mastered it so well. Offense, too, is an art he had to relearn, for once he reached the NBA, size alone did not allow him to toss up short jumpers, to bank rebounds, or to capitalize to any appreciable degree on the "garbage" shots that result from offensive rebounds in college basketball. "You have to work for your points up here," he admits, "while a big man in college sort of finds them coming his way during the course of a game."

In his rookie season, Walk averaged only 8.2 points per game, while playing an average of just sixteen minutes per game, one-third of the maximum playing time. "It was tough," he said. "I wasn't much of an offensive threat. I just wasn't there yet as a pure shooter, and I wasn't experienced enough to make the openings happen or to hold my own on defense."

But, being the type who takes immediate action to correct deficiencies, Neal embarked on a program of weightlifting, swimming, running, and basketball as soon as the season ended, a regimen that demanded a full five days of each week. "I had to get myself accustomed to the long schedule," he said. "In college, we played twenty, maybe twenty-five games in an entire season, so there is no way to really be ready for the length of an NBA season."

Walk's preoccupation with his basketball future is indicative of the dedication he has to the sport. "If I am going to stay in the NBA," he says, "I do not want to be just a fringe player. I want to help, to contribute. Sure, there is a personal pride and self-satisfaction involved, but if I can't help my team, I don't think I'd be happy sitting on the bench. So I had a lot of improving to do for the next season. Weights and running can build strength and stamina, but you have to play the game all year against top competition to stay mentally sharp. That is just as important as good body condition."

Walk encountered problems when, as a rookie, he had to cover such centers as Nate Thurmond, Wilt Chamberlain, Willis Reed—strong, experienced men who are the key ingredients in the success their teams have known.

"Every center in the league gave me trouble my rookie year," Walk says. "Why? Because they're all so good. You just don't realize how good they are until you have to work against them. You can't imagine how strong some of those men are and what good shooters they are. The day of the big center who is out there just for his rebounding is gone. Centers in today's NBA are as quick as forwards, and they can shoot just as well. But they are so much bigger and stronger. I have to get that way too, and confidence helps a lot."

But, in the case of Neal Walk, there is much to work with. In his rookie season, for example, he made an average of five rebounds per game in one-third of the possible playing time; therefore, he could be projected as a fifteen-rebounds-a-game performer, a figure he nearly reached in his second season, when he was the team's second highest rebounder.

More dramatic, however, was Neal's sudden emergence as a scorer. After the 8.2 point average as a rookie, Walk spent the second season hovering at a figure nearly double that. He became the Suns' fourth leading scorer, behind such proven point-producers as Dick Van Arsdale, Connie Hawkins, and Clem Haskins.

"The difference in Walk is astonishing," says coach Fitzsimmons. "When I took over as coach, all I could go on was his first season. I knew he had ability, and I knew he was going to improve, but to be perfectly frank I was surprised at just how quickly he did improve. His progress was very gratifying. He really worked at it."

Walk has always worked for whatever success he has found on the basketball court. In his college days at the University of Florida, he was thought of, at least in the beginning, as a somewhat slow bigman. Too slow, they said, for the NBA.

So he worked to build up his speed.

"Running helps," he says, "not only for muscle conditoning and leg strength but for wind. The stronger you are, the harder you can play, and the more wind you have, the longer you can play."

His scoring in college was never a problem, nor was his stature as one of the NCAA's leading major-college rebounders. In fact, during his junior year (the 1967–1968 season), he was the only player in the nation to rank among the top ten in both scoring and rebounding. Neal averaged 26.5 points and 19.8 rebounds per game in the twenty-five games the Gators played. His rebounding record led the nation. He maintained his skill during his senior year, when he averaged twenty-four points and 18.5 rebounds, taking the Gators to an 18–9 regular season record and a spot in the National Invitation Tournament in New York's Madison Square Garden.

Walk's college coach, Tommy Bartlett, an innovator and one of the brightest coaches in the fiercely competitive Southeastern Conference, recalls Neal's contributions to the team.

"He was the finest all-around bigman I have ever coached," Bartlett says, "and with the obvious exception of Alcindor, he was absolutely the best bigman in the country in his junior and senior seasons. He could score and rebound. He could play tough defense. His team leadership abilities increased his overall value, too, since he was able to lift the team both with his performance and his personality. I've never known a more determined competitor. As coaching material, he was ideal.

"He learned things quickly, and he never failed to understand even the most sophisticated strategy or tactics. It will be a great task trying to equal our record now that Neal has graduated, but we were able to accomplish a lot with him and some of it, I hope, rubbed off on the freshmen and sophomores who knew him."

In Bartlett's somewhat unique offensive jargon, Walk had been Florida's low post man. His duties involved rebounding and scoring to such an extent that he was expected to be the team leader in both categories. Walk came through magnificiently. "He was perfect. The low post man should be the team's tallest player and best rebounder," Bartlett explains. "He should have a good short hook shot with either hand. He should be able to score consistently from close up. He must be able to interchange with the high post man and screen for the outside shooters. He is, on defense, the key man in the 1–3–1 zone defense at the foul line. He must be able to clog up the middle and obtain strong rebounding position quickly."

Neal Walk did all of this and more. "He became the ideal low post man," Bartlett says, "a pleasure to watch."

Low post, under Bartlett's system, involves playing on either side of the foul lane, close in to the basket. If this sounds familiar when compared to Neal's style as a pro, it should.

"It is what I am most comfortable doing," Neal says, "and it seems to have a place in the pro game."

So, too, does Neal Walk. And all those detractors who scoffed when his name followed that of Lew Alcindor are now the first to agree.

"I worked with Walk all summer," Jim Fox recalls. "The summer before he played as a rookie, we worked in Phoenix almost every day. Man-to-man. He's big and strong and moves well for a man his size. It will just be a matter of time and learning, but he'll make it."

He did. Score one for the "second best" center in the country.

Larry Wiese is the head coach of basketball at St. Bonaventure College in Olean, New York. During the dramatic year of Bob Lanier's senior season, Wiese sat down with a man at an awards banquet and spoke about his star.

"You show me a man who has found something Bob Lanier cannot do on a court," Wiese said, "and I will show you either a liar or a fool. There is nothing he cannot do, and that goes for bringing the ball downcourt, too, if he has to."

Since Bob Lanier is 6'11" and weighs between 265 and 280 pounds, Wiese's statement was instantly written off as the well-intentioned words of a staunchly loyal man. A short time later, however, Wiese's dinner companion had occasion to watch St. Bonaventure in the NCAA tournament against Davidson and actually saw this tree trunk of an athlete dribble the full length of the court, pestered by a guard or two.

He was pestered, but he was not bothered. There is a difference in semantics that helps to explain the talent of Lanier and the commendable attitude he displays in playing the game he has chosen to dominate.

There have been heroes at St. Bonaventure, All-America players before Bob Lanier—Tom Stith, Freddy Crawford, and Whitey Martin, for examples. But none of them hit the game with the same impact as did this gigantic young man, this Gulliver trapped in a world of collegiate Lilliputians.

Because of its location and its history of several time-honored rivalries with other local upstate New York schools, St. Bonaventure does not play the high-powered schedule of some of the basketball factories masquerading as universities in this country. There are games with Niagara and Seton Hall, Iona and Canisius, but these schools do not normally figure in national rankings. Nor do they attract the necessary manpower to cope with All-America players, especially with All-Americas who dominate both ends of the court, who seem to cover both ends at once, who appear to travel the distance from basket to basket in three or four strides.

Thus for a long time newspaper reporters underrated the real value of Bob Lanier, choosing to mask it instead in the subterfuge of a lower level of competition. Nothing could have been further from the truth. True, Bob Lanier seldom found an opponent even close to his size. True, his girth, carried with the deceptive grace so many very large men possess, kept the enemy easily at bay. True, his ability to shoot from great distances with accuracy was not miraculous, and it was easy for him to stand under the basket and redirect the errant shots of his teammates and to take defensive rebounds without having to leap to the full extent of his ability.

But Bob Lanier's talent was legitimate, and because it was, St. Bonaventure soon began playing in a more competitive cricle of teams. Lanier took the Bonnies to an NCAA tournament, and there he was the dominant figure until a freak fall in a game with Villanova resulted in torn knee ligaments in his right leg.

He underwent emergency surgery the next day. While his knee recovered, he was unable to practice and thus to stay in shape. As a result, his rookie season with the Detroit Pistons (1970–1971) was less brilliant than had been expected.

"Let me tell you something," offered Eddie Donovan, now the general manager of the Buffalo Braves and then the general manager of the New York Knicks, "there is no better bigman in the country than Bob Lanier. He has as much strength as Willis Reed, and while he might not know how to use it yet, as Willis does, he will learn very quickly when he starts to play in the NBA.

"I have never seen a man that big with his shooting touch besides Willis, and if this sounds as though I'm comparing him to Reed, you're right. I am. Only Bob is bigger. He's the best to come along in Willis' mold since Willis himself, and he is good enough to make it tough even for Alcindor, too."

Lanier and Alcindor never met on a collegiate court, but Lanier often spoke about playing against Alcindor. He did so with a gleam in his eyes and a childlike excitement.

"Now there's a challenge," he said, when still in college. "I know he is quicker than I am, yet I don't think he's any stronger. I don't think he'd be able to jump over me if I got position on rebounds. Could I score against him? Yes. To be a player, you must have confidence in your own ability. I feel I would be able to score against a tenfooter. If he lets me have the outside shots, I'll take 'em and make 'em. If he comes out to me, I'll muscle him inside. I'm really looking forward to playing him."

Lanier's rookie season in the NBA, however, was a disappointment for him and for the Pistons, who had outbid the ABA's New York Nets to the tune of a $1.4 million contract to sign him. The knee surgery suffered in the Eastern Regional finals had affected his agility and stamina, but the damage was not permanent. His inability to continue working strenuously had caused him to put on weight, but this was likewise only a temporary problem.

The Pistons were so confident of his ability that general manager Edward Coil offered Lanier the staggering contract in Buffalo General Hospital, where Lanier was recuperating from surgery. "His lawyer was late," Coil laughs, "and we were alone for a while. This kid is so sharp he got more money out of me while we waited."

Detroit's head coach, Bill van Breda Kolff, was far too impressed with Lanier to allow an injury to dissuade him from making Bob the team's first draft choice—the first man chosen in the 1970 selections.

"You can always tell when you have a special one," van Breda Kolff said early in Lanier's rookie season. The coach should know all about special ones, since he was the head coach at Princeton when Bill Bradley stood the country on its ear. "How? You know, people start telling other people all the things he can't do. They can't find anything wrong with his basic game, so they begin analyzing all the little things that any rookie would be weak in. They say he can't use his left hand, he can't rebound, he can't run, he can't do this, and he can't do that. All I know is that he started out for us averaging twenty-three minutes a game, scoring twenty points, and grabbing a bunch of important rebounds. There aren't too many veteran players in the league who can do that, let alone rookies.

"Bob has good hands. He passes well, and he is a fine shooter. He has a good knowledge of the game. If there is any doubt about his game, it's his ability to run hard and his quickness. But this is common with all rookies. You always wonder if they can take the grind. So far he has. His knee doesn't seem to bother him on offense, but it has hampered his defense and rebounding a bit."

Lanier, an intelligent, well-spoken man with a quick and contagious smile, confessed to real worry about his knee. He added, however, that it never became a serious problem.

"It doesn't swell up much," he said. "All that summer after I had signed, I worried. I wasn't able to run, you know, and I sure couldn't play any ball, and I got flabby and out of condition. I just didn't keep up. I was away from basketball for five months. It was hard work, but it came back. I guess I'll always remember the fall I took in rookie camp. I guess the coach will too."

The fall occurred during a scrimmage at Ypsilanti, Michigan, the Pistons' summer training site. Lanier tripped over rookie guard Harvey Marlatt. Teammates said they heard "a lot of pops" coming from his injured right knee as Bob's massive frame slammed down on the court. The players were silent, stunned, fearful that this career had ended before it had really begun.

But the fall turned out to be a blessing. The "pops" were the sounds of adhesions tearing loose. Adhesions are a form of scar tissue that forms after knee surgery. They provide protection while the knee is healing, but eventually they must break free if full mobility is to be restored. Usually this process is drawn out and painful.

"Bob broke them all in one day," van Breda Kolff

says. "He was lucky. The doctor said they usually go one
at a time. He was better off for it in the long run, but I
guess all our hearts stopped beating for a minute until he
got up."

Once that shock was over and Lanier saw that his knee
was sound, he progressed rapidly. "I played Willis Reed
in an exhibition game shortly after," he recalls. "I thought
we were pretty evenly matched." So did Reed.

Bob has always worked hard to improve his game. As
a collegian, he set certain goals for each season and concentrated on achieving them. "I wasn't much of a shooter
when I first came to St. Bonaventure," Lanier said. "So I
tried to see if I could increase my scoring each year. I
did. Now I take a special pride in being able to make long
shots."

Sure enough, Lanier's figures did move steadily higher,
from 26.2 points per game as a sophomore to 27.2 as a
junior and 29.1 as a senior.

"Also, I was kind of overweight and slow when I was a
sophomore," he says, "and so I couldn't get down on offense fast enough. As a result, I missed getting more rebounds. So I tried to improve my speed and my rebounding in each season with the varsity."

Lanier's rebounding figures did indeed increase. He
had a total of 390 as a sophomore (15.6 per game), 16.1
as a junior, and 17.2 as a senior. He scored more than
two thousand points as a collegian, pulled down 1,180 rebounds in his three-year career, and finished with an
amazing 57.6 percent field goal accuracy figure. Twice he
was a unanimous All-America selection, despite the presence of Alcindor on all the honor teams in Bob's junior
year.

Lanier was the most sought after collegian in the nation when he had finished his career, and both leagues began bombarding him with offers. "The NBA," he said,

"had always been my first choice. I listened to the ABA people because it would have been rude not to, but I wanted the NBA all along. With people like Reed and Alcindor and Nate Thurmond and Wes Unseld, I just had to see how I stacked up."

According to his mates on the Pistons, Lanier "stacks up" just fine. Guard Dave Bing, one of the most prolific scorers the league has known, had reason to rejoice after watching Bob a few times. "I guess his first game really was enough for me to see what he could do," Bing recalls. "We had blown a seventeen-point lead and led by only nine in the fourth quarter when the coach put him in. It was his first pro game. I'm pretty sure we were thinking that he wouldn't be able to do it. I know I was. It was a big load the coach put on him in his first game, but Bob came through. Just give him one turn around this league, and he'll be one of the greatest. Everyone knows how good he is, and if they don't, they'll soon find out. We have needed a really good bigman since I've been with the Pistons. It looks like we finally found him. With Bob in there, we believe in ourselves.

"I don't remember when it was, but we were playing the Bucks, and we were behind by seven points with less than two minutes to play. I looked around and I saw all our fans going home. That was when I said to myself, 'They're wrong, they should stick around, we're not finished yet.' And we won. Bob was a big factor in stopping Alcindor. He really came through for us."

As a rookie, Lanier was paired with 6'10" Otto Moore, but as the season wore on, van Breda Kolff began to send in his prized rookie more often when the going was rough.

"Lanier plays Alcindor as well as anybody is going to play him," the coach said. "This may only be Lewie's second year in the league, but he's already the dominant player. But Lanier is working at it, and he is really coach-able. He's not just some big overgrown kid. He has moves, and he knows what to do. He's been able to 'lean' on Alcindor a little more than smaller centers, but if the officials start blowing the whistle, he can stick with him man-to-man and make him take uncomfortable shots."

Lanier himself, looking back at his first pro season, was far from satisfied. "I was not ready," he says, "because of my knee. But I saw what the pro game is like, and I was convinced I could handle it. I have a lot to learn, but I don't think I'll disappoint anyone. Alcindor? He was ev-erything I expected. He was able to beat me laterally coming across in front of the basket. I'll have to learn more about him, I guess."

Bob Lanier knew for a long time that he wanted to try professional basketball. "I went to a lot of Willis Reed's summer camps," he smiles, "but Willis made me play with some of the pros. I didn't think I'd have any major problems once I saw I could hold my own with them."

Lanier finished as the third highest scorer on the Pis-tons in his rookie year, behind the incomparable back-court duo of Bing and Jimmy Walker. He waged a neck-and-neck battle with Moore for team rebounding honors, a contest Lanier finally won at the end of the season. His scoring was better than fifteen points per game, and his rebounds came at the rate of just under ten per outing. It was an auspicious start for a partially hampered rookie striving to keep up with the best pros in the game while nursing a knee that was still stiff and tender.

"It taught me determination," he smiles. "I learned not to let the pain affect my outlook on the game. I'm sure next season will be better. I know all this experience will have to help me. And my leg will be sound."

Van Breda Kolff adds: "He'll make us a winner, a big winner . . . and soon. This is the kind of a kid who can't miss becoming a superstar. He's the kind you find on All-Star teams every year, the kind you compare with Alcindor."

High praise? Not at all. It is a fair evaluation of Bob Lanier.

Only one other guard had been drafted, Pete Maravich, when the Portland Trail Blazers announced their selection in the 1970 college player draft. Still available were Calvin Murphy of Niagara, Mike Price of Illinois, Jimmy Collins of New Mexico State, John Vallely of UCLA, and Rex Morgan of Jacksonville.

Whom did the Trail Blazers choose?

"Geoff Petrie, Princeton," intoned Stu Inman, Portland's director of player personnel.

"Who?" asked fans of the team, since Portland is far removed from the rural New Jersey campus of Princeton. "Did he say Princeton? Isn't that a sissy school back East?"

Inman did say Princeton, and he had been hoping that Petrie would still be available when the Trail Blazers' turn came up. "We even tried to figure out a sample draft a few days before the real one," a team spokesman explains, "just to see which teams needed a guard and which ones we thought they might take. We kind of knew Atlanta would take Maravich. They had to, to keep him in the league. But we knew all about Geoff, and if we did, everyone else did, too. It was a great moment. We had been tense, waiting to see who each team picked and hoping not to hear his name called."

Petrie, then, was the eighth player picked, and he was either the first or the second guard chosen, depending on your version of the Maravich-Atlanta situation. What was there that caused to much excitement? How could a kid from that "sissy school back East" elicit such praise from seasoned pro basketball men?

"It was easy," Inman says. "Petrie was the best guard in the country. I don't care who you include. Throw in any name you like, but Geoff was the best."

Petrie was not the stereotyped version of the Ivy League athlete, the spoiled son of a millionaire business-man. The Ivy schools, having savored the publicity, noto-riety, and success brought to them by Bill Bradley, vowed to obtain more such heroes.

Columbia had turned out several since the Bradley era, including Jim McMillian (drafted by the Los Angeles Lakers on the same first round as Petrie), Dave New-mark (who played for Atlanta and the ABA Carolina Courgars), and Heywood Dotson (who accepted a Rhodes Scholarship in lieu of pro basketball). Princeton had produced John Hummer, a 6'9" forward-center tak-en by Buffalo on that same first round. Other Ivy League schools have stepped up their recruiting and interest in basketball; as a result, there are several talented players currently operating in the Ivy League who are considered pro potential.

But not since Bradley, perhaps, has a player impressed the pros quite as profoundly as Petrie, a High School All-America from Springfield, Pennsylvania, who had been recruited by "oh, about one hundred or so schools" before deciding to attend Princeton. He had listened to most of the high-powered recruiting pitches from the At-lantic Coast Conference, the SEC, the Big Ten, and the major independents, and all were equally hopeful of land-ing him. "I just wasn't sure," he remembers. "Then I met a man who really talked to me like a man, who talked about education too."

The man was Bill van Breda Kolff, who later left Prince-ton to become the head coach of the Los Angeles Lakers and who ultimately left the Lakers to take a similar job coaching the Pistons—and Bob Lanier. "I guess when I saw that Princeton was interested in me, that made up my mind," Petrie says. "Education has always been my goal. I wanted the best preparation possible. And with the reputation Princeton had as a winning basketball team, I was sure of playing high caliber competition. Princeton plays a national schedule and plays in tournaments, and lots of pro scouts have started to watch the team. You'd be surprised at the level of play in the Ivy League. I don't think there's a conference in the country much better."

So Geoff Petrie went to Princeton. As a freshman he showed all the talent and potential van Breda Kolff knew he had. He was a feared scorer, for his long-range jumper was already famous. But his height (6′4″) enabled him to rebound with the bigger players and to penetrate deeper with the ball and shoot over smaller guards.

He improved game by game as a playmaker and a passer, and his overall development caused van Breda Kolff to note: "If anybody can come close to what Bill Bradley did, it just might be this kid."

But van Breda Kolff did not witness the varsity career of Petrie. He was offered the job with the Lakers, and in early 1967 he accepted it. He did, however, recommend his successor at Princeton, the man who had before replaced him at Lafayette, little Pete Carril.

It was Carril, then, who was able to work with Petrie and bask in the glow of his emergence as a great player. It was Carril who took the Tigers to a 20–6 record in his first season, with an Ivy League mark that tied with Columbia for the championship. Petrie was a valuable weapon in that crusade, averaging 12.9 points and 4.5 rebounds per game. "Geoff was able to do anything a basketball player has to do," Carril remembers. "He was quick enough to beat other guards and strong enough to

play with forwards. He was smart, and he won games
with his passing and playmaking. Yet we knew he was
going to become better."

He did. In his junior year, the 1968–1969 season,
Princeton was 19–7. They captured another Ivy championship, and Geoff Petrie had put it all together. He averaged 20.8 points (scoring 541 total) and increased his
rebounding and assists figures. He earned a second consecutive All-Ivy League nomination, a position on the All-
East team, and honorable mention on several All-America squads. He had become the complete player, and there
was a season still remaining.

His senior year, however, did not turn out to be as successful as everyone felt it would. Petrie suffered a freak-
ish injury—he pulled a back muscle and a spinal disc
leaning over a billiards table in a Princeton clubroom. As
a result, he missed the Tigers' first six games.

"That wasn't all of it, though," Carril reminds. "When
he did come back, he wasn't really ready to play. He had
lost his timing and his shooting eye, and he had to run to
get his legs in shape. I don't think he ever hit 100 percent
peak that season, and it was a darn shame, because he
might have been absolutely impossible to stop. As it was,
he played pretty well, though, didn't he?"

Petrie, in the twenty games he did play, scored 445
points, for a 22.3 average. He recovered 120 rebounds,
for an average of six per game. Princeton did not successfully defend its Ivy League crown, losing to Pennsylvania,
but the Tigers earned a respectable 16–9 record, bringing
Carril his third straight winning season and a three-year
record of 55–22. "Petrie was just a pleasure to coach," he
says. "He knew exactly what had to be done. He had
enormous talent. I don't see how he can fail in the NBA."

Petrie has not failed. Indeed, he has never even come
close to failing.

"I always wanted pro ball," he says, "and when Portland drafted me so high, I was the happiest kid in the world. I never thought it would be the first round. I was just hoping for a chance in the pros."

Geoff made the cross-country trip to Portland and was introduced to Rolland Todd, the new head coach of this first-year expansion franchise. He knew right away that it was going to be a pleasant relationship. "Coach Todd has certain theories about this game," Petrie told a reporter early in his rookie season. "He feels the fast break is the best offense and that a team in top condition can run and shoot all night. I liked that just fine."

And so it began. Todd took a few weeks to study Petrie and knew he was going to be special. "He'll start," Todd said. "If I don't know anything else about this team, I know Geoff Petrie will start. And I know he'll star in this league."

The season began, and from the very first week, Geoff's name led the Trail Blazers in the scoring column. Slowly he crept up to the list of NBA leaders until his average per game, which was more than twenty-two points, placed him in the NBA's top ten, ahead of such scorers as Chet Walker, Willis Reed, Dick Van Arsdale, and Lennie Wilkens.

Around the league, they began describing the Blazers as the finest of the three new expansion teams (Cleveland and Buffalo were the other two), and they began talking about Geoff Petrie, about his scoring, his defense, and his poise, which far exceeded that of most rookies.

"He just doesn't know he's a rookie," Todd said. "He just gets out there and does what has to be done. This is a fine player. He is pure basketball, and my admiration for the job his coaches did in college is great. He came to us ready to play, and I have to feel he is the finest rookie guard in the country. When it became clear that he would have to score a lot of points in our offense, it never once shook him. He just went out and started shooting, and the veterans, who might have resented it, began to look for him. They realized he was a special kind of rookie, the kind who can step in and do the job right away. He's been one of the major reasons for any success we might have had here."

Petrie did his job so well that by the middle of the season he was one of two rookies voted to the NBA All-Star team. Cleveland's John Johnson, also a first round pick, was the other. Geoff played a total of five minutes in the All-Star game, and while he did not score, he contributed one assist and accounted for three blocked or stolen passes. It was an adequate showing for the rookie from Princeton. At the conclusion of the season, he shared, with Cowens, the Rookie of the Year award.

"Just being on that team was enough for me," he said happily. "I didn't think I had a chance. After all, the guards in this league are all so great I never even thought about me on the team. I was surprised and shocked. Yes, I guess I was amazed at it all. This seems kind of unreal. I mean, last year I was playing against Cornell and Brown, and now, just a year later, it's the Lakers and the Knicks and the Bucks. It is kind of hard to believe, isn't it?"

Perhaps it is for Geoff Petrie, but it is not for Stu Inman and Rolland Todd.

"Next year," Todd says, "I think Geoff will be an All-Star starter. He just can't be stopped now, and this year of experience should put him over the top."

The kid from the "sissy school back East" has made it. All the way.

When the Boston Celtics approached the 1970 draft,

they did so with a desperate need for a center. Not since Bill Russell had left basketball to pursue a Hollywood career had the Celtics been able to field the dominant bigman in the middle, essential to any team with championship aspirations. They had tried several, but no one had worked out.

As a result, the Celtics of 1969–1970 had failed to make the NBA playoffs for the first time in twenty years. During that time this famous team had won a remarkable eleven league championships and had established a reign of domination unparalleled in professional athletics.

It was a rather unnerving experience to look at the lineup of playoff teams without seeing the name of the Boston Celtics. It was even more shattering to Red Auerbach, the former coach and now general manager and vice-president of the Celtics. And it was a crushing blow to Tom Heinsohn, the first-year head coach who, as an All-Star forward, had been a part of many of those victorious years.

"We need a bigman," Auerbach said grimly during that season. "We cannot win without one. A bigman is what we need, and a bigman is what we have to get. I do not intend for the Boston Celtics to become just another team. We'll find our bigman."

Then Red took his charts, scouting reports, and cigars and went to the New York offices of the NBA, where the draft was being conducted.

The first bigman, the one every team wanted, was Bob Lanier, but he was gone when the first team announced its selection. There were others, of course, and it was generally felt that Boston would either take Sam Lacey of New Mexico State or try to trade.

Auerbach, picking fourth, made his announcement. "The Boston Celtics take center Dave Cowens of Florida State."

"Isn't he a forward, Red?" asked a reporter.

"No, sir," Red responded. "He is a center. The best one around."

And so Dave Cowens became a member of the Celtics. At 6'9" and 230 pounds, he was going to be asked to give away up to five inches per match-up and hold down the center spot on a fabled team trying to recapture its glory. But old Red was shrewd. Surely he was planning to "make do" with Cowens at center for the 1970–1971 season. Later he would draft a real bigman, and Dave would move to forward, his natural position.

Right? Wrong. "Nothing doing," Auerbach said. "Dave Cowens is a center. Our center. He will be as good as any, and it won't take him a long time, either."

Dave Cowens is not big. In fact, there are some forwards who are taller—and quicker. But none of them are any stronger, nor are any of them more determined to succeed. About midway through his rookie season, Cowens made a statement that provided an indication of his pride. "I wish they'd stop calling me a rookie," he said. "I am not a rookie any longer. I have already played nearly as many games as I did in three years at Florida State. I'm stronger than I was then, and I'm faster. I have had to play against guys who are sometimes so much bigger than I that I look straight at their shoulders. But it's all been working for us, and I don't think it's fair to call any first year player who has been starting a rookie."

No one would argue with at least one of the points Cowens made. He did not play like a rookie.

"He is a big, graceful man and a great player," Auerbach says. "But he's not really much bigger than many forwards. I don't necessarily feel you need a mountain in the middle to win. Look how much Baltimore has done with Wes Unseld at center, and he's only 6'8". But very strong. And look at what the Knicks have done with Willis Reed. He's only 6′9″. You can win in other ways—the way we used to do it with the Celtics, for instance. Other guys have to help out on the boards. Sometimes a bigman can slow down a running offense like the Celtics use. A team can get top-heavy with a too-big center. Too much size can be a hindrance."

Something else about Cowens impressed Auerbach. "Dave is a very dedicated kid," he added. "A dedicated kid isn't unheard of, but there aren't too many of them left. We have to stop Dave from doing too much. He would burn himself out in practice and all during the summer if we didn't keep an eye on him. We have only one problem, telling him when to lay off. He does too much. By midseason he made them forget Pete Maravich, right? He meant more to us than Pistol Pete did to the Atlanta Hawks."

Cowens is not overly surprised at his success, but he does find surprise in the effect his success has had on others. "In the beginning of the season," he said, "I was getting something like twenty rebounds a game. Then they began leaning on me."

When the really big centers begin to fear a rookie, they use their bulk, which is usually more than 260 pounds, to muscle him underneath, to keep him away from the boards. "You have to learn to play tough every night in the pros, or you can get murdered," Dave responds. "I'm taking a physical beating, but I'm learning fast. I'm playing more than I dreamed I would as a rookie, and my main practice work involves defense. People who say they don't play defense in the NBA need a mental examination. You can bet they do."

As a rookie, Cowens was one of the few men in the league ranking in high double figures in both scoring and rebounding. "If Cowens isn't the rookie of the year," said Heinsohn, "he'll be robbed. Cowens is a pro. He's a 6'9" John Havlicek. He's always moving, always hustling, up on the boards, stealing passes. He's so quick for a big man it's almost uncanny, and he has a great knack for tap-ins. Most kids bring the ball back down, then go up with it. Not Dave. He seems to hang up there long enough to tap the ball down. It's quicker to score that way—the baskets come easier."

Cowens' shooting is another plus, according to Heinsohn. "He can hit from thirty feet away. There is only one forward I can think of on our team who is faster. Dave gets way up there when he rebounds, like he has springs in his legs. He hits the boards all the time, never gives up. But his shooting is a surprise. I knew when we looked at him in college that he could become a good shooter, but once you start playing in the pros those shots seem tougher to make. But Dave likes to shoot long, and if we need him to do it, he does. He's just great. He'll do whatever has to be done to win."

Cowens earned several honors at Florida State, including a few All-America credits, but he had never considered the Seminoles when it was time to pick a school. "I always thought about playing for Kentucky," he says, "but Adolph Rupp had already named his dozen or so freshmen scholarships when he sent me a letter. I was a little disappointed. I guess he wasn't too interested in me. I had heard from teams like Western Kentucky, Cincinnati, Louisville, North Texas and Florida State.

"I guess I chose Florida State because coach Hugh Durham impressed me. He said I would start as a sophomore, and I wanted that. I didn't much like the idea of sitting on the bench until a star center graduated."

Cowens' rebounding was good enough in his three var-

sity seasons to rank him no lower than eighth (as a sophomore) in the NCAA's statistics yearly. He averaged 17
caroms as a sophomore, 17.5 as a junior, and 17.2 as a
senior, finishing sixth and fourth, respectively, in his last
two seasons. His scoring never suffered. Dave amassed
1,479 points as a varsity performer, averaging 18.8, 20.3,
and 17.3 for the three years. As a senior, he was the main
force behind the only victory any team achieved over
Jacksonville when he gave away four inches to All-America center Artis Gilmore and ran the pants off him.

"I wasn't sure I could make it as a college player," he
admits now. "But I knew I had to have a college education. I didn't start playing in high school until my junior
year (at Newport Catholic High). I guess I was meant to
be a basketball player because I grew five inches, from
6'1" to 6'6" between my sophomore and junior years.
I played on both the jayvees and the varsity when I was a
junior, but it didn't bother me much. In fact, I think it
helped to develop me faster."

In three Florida State seasons with Cowens at center,
the Seminoles' record was 59–19. He majored in crimi-
nology. "I tried business school first," he says, "but I had
a terrible time, particularly when I lost so much class time
to basketball trips. I had to decide if I wanted basketball
to be my life, and when I discovered it was what I wanted, I switched to a major I liked instead."

Cowens' first taste of pro competition came during the
summer following his graduation, when he was invited to
play in the annual Maurice Stokes Memorial Game at a
well-known resort hotel in the Catskills. All the top
names were there—Willis Reed, Wilt Chamberlain, Billy
Cunningham, Pete Maravich. But it was Dave Cowens
who stole the show. It was Dave who scored thirty-two
points, and it was Dave who pulled down twenty-two rebounds—without playing the full game.

Auerbach, one of the two honorary coaches for the game, had Cowens on his team. He was thrilled with the performance his rookie turned in. "I sent him in near the end of the first quarter," he said. "He started to rebound, block shots, muscle his way in for tip-ins, and hustle up and down the court. I just had to leave him in to see what he could do."

Dave DeBusschere of the Knicks, one of the top three forwards in the game and surely the strongest, has much to say about Dave Cowens. "He is big, strong, and he runs well," Dave begins. "He hits the boards as hard as anyone, and he always seems to be in great shape. He's very, very quick. He sure looks like a good one. I don't think I've seen a rookie center play quite like him. We knew what Alcindor was going to do, and Dave seems to have to work so much harder to accomplish his goals. Yes, he is as intense as Havlicek, and I guess that's just about the highest compliment I could pay any rookie."

Red-haired Dave Cowens, the center who wasn't supposed to be, has turned the Celtics into a dynamic team again. If he continues to improve, there is no telling how far the Celtics can go. "Remember, we were just a bunch of good players until we got Bill Russell," says Heinsohn. "It seems to be shaping up like that all over again. We had a bunch of good players—and then we got Dave Cowens."

One year before Dave Cowens, the Celtics had a guard of great ability and high potential. His name is Jo Jo White.

The success of the Celtics would not have been achieved without their string of perfect guards. Sam Jones, K. C. Jones, Bob Cousy, Bill Sharman, and Larry

Siegfried left their imprint on the record books and in the playoffs. Suddenly, however, the Celtics found themselves without top guards. The Jones boys retired, and Cousy and Sharman had long since departed: Siegfried was plucked by San Diego in a trade. Boston was left with very few capable backcourt men and the offense, without the scoring potential and leadership of a dynamic backcourt, became ordinary—a word never before used to define the Celtics.

Auerbach went to the draft meetings of 1969, not in a position to pick early and high, as he did in 1970, but holding the last choice in each round because of the Celtics' championship victory in the playoffs. It had taken a seven-game playoff series with the Lakers, after successfully fighting back the initial charge of the budding champions in New York, but the Celtics, under Russell, had won yet another league championship.

This was, of course, wonderful for the fans and for the team, but it was not very rewarding when it was time to strengthen the squad through drafting. The team that chooses last, they say, might as well pick girls.

"We need a guard," Auerbach said. "There are two or three I would take. There is one I absolutely want. I hope he is still available when we draft."

There were good guards that year, including Butch Beard of Louisville, Mike Davis of Virginia Union, Herm Gilliam of Purdue, Willie McCarter of Drake, Johnny Warren of St. John's, and Lucious Allen of UCLA. And Jo Jo White of Kansas.

"White can't shoot with the pros," said most of the scouts. "He just won't be enough of a scorer to make it."

Auerbach said nothing. But when it came time for him to announce the Boston selection, he fairly trembled with excitement. "We made it," he said. "We'll take Jo Jo White."

According to a reliable source, Auerbach had written the name of the guard he wanted on a piece of paper and had given it to a local reporter, with the instruction not to open it until after the Celtics had made their choice. When the man did open it, he saw the name Jo Jo White.

White is a 6'3", 190-pound native of St. Louis. He had been a truly outstanding performer at Kansas. But playing for the innovative Ted Owens, Jo Jo never had to be a high-scoring guard, a fact that many of the scouts obviously failed to note. Owens likes a deliberate, controlled style of offense, which has proven successful for him in the tough Big Eight Conference.

The key to it all is one great guard. "I need one guy," Owens says, "who controls the ball most of the game. He takes it upcourt and makes most of the passes and runs the offense. He calls plays and directs the other four guys and sets up whatever he thinks will work. He must pass well and dribble well. I guess he is more of a quarterback than a guard, isn't he?"

He was exactly that, a quarterback. He left the scoring to such guns as Roger Bohnensteil, Dave Nash, and Dave Robisch, while he piled up assists and played a stifling brand of defense that almost always held the opponents' high scorer to considerably less than his average.

"Defense? I don't think there's a man in the country who can get away from Jo Jo," Owens says, "and I don't think any of those high-scoring hotshots would be able to get anything near what they do against other people. He has been the finest defensive guard I've ever seen."

After a high school career at McKinley in St. Louis, Jo Jo tried to maintain his reputation as a scorer when he enrolled at Kansas. But he saw it was not necessary. Kansas was good enough to win the Big Eight and qualify for the automatic spot in the NCAA tournament reserved for the conference champion.

Then Jo Jo suffered a traumatic experience. Playing in the Mid-West final against the ultimate national champion, Texas Western, Kansas earned a tie with one second left on the clock. And Jo Jo had the ball. From roughly thirty-five feet away, he took a long jumper, and it swished through the nets as the buzzer sounded. But joy turned to ashes seconds later, when an official signalled that Jo Jo had stepped on the out-of-bounds line. The basket did not count, and an overtime session was necessary. Texas Western won by a single point.

"I don't remember ever feeling so bad," Jo Jo said. "We had it won. I made the shot. But if the man said my foot was on the line, I guess it was. All I could think of after that was that somehow I had let my teammates down."

So Jo Jo White went from shooter and scorer to passer and playmaker. "I liked it better that way," he said. "We had the big guys who could score more easily, and if I had a talent for passing and setting up the offensive plays, it would have been selfish of me to take too many shots."

His defense and his playmaking, however, helped him gain several All-America honorable mention awards and a place on the All-Star Big Eight Conference team. It also earned him an international reputation and international acclaim. Jo Jo played on the Pan-American Games team in Japan between his junior and senior seasons, and he was a member of the 1968 United States Olympic team that won the Gold Medal in Mexico City.

In his junior season, Kansas narrowly missed another Big Eight crown, losing out by one game to Kansas State. An invitation to play in the National Invitation Tournament in New York soothed that wound, however, and Jo Jo took his team to the final game before Kansas fell to

Dayton, paced by All-America forward Donnie May.

Jo Jo has a peculiar affinity for basketball that transcends a normal interest in the game. He has a theory about "playing with a basketball" a certain number of hours each day. "You know, just dribbling it and passing it and controlling it. Just holding it, too, I guess, is part of it."

This single-mindedness of purpose led to a comical answer to a serious question asked of him when he returned from Japan. He had experienced a once-in-a-lifetime trip to the Orient as a guest of that country, and he was asked, upon his return to the United States, his impressions of Japan.

"Well," he said, totally serious, "it's all right, I guess. But the climate isn't too good for basketball. The moisture in the air affects the basketball courts, and the ball doesn't bounce true."

His impressions of a foreign country were thus expressed completely in terms of basketball. His comment provides a revealing indication of the motivation of Jo Jo White.

Several factors delayed his professional debut at the start of the 1969–1970 season, including a stint in the marines and a series of minor injuries. He missed all of the team's precious pre-season period and the first twenty games of the regulation schedule. When he was finally available, the lost time proved enough to interfere with his progress in learning and mastering the Celtics' complex system.

Despite his delay, he finished the season as the team's fifth-leading scorer (729 points and a 12.2 average for sixty games). He won a starting job by late January, and from then on his scoring average was well over twenty points per game.

His defense, as always, was remarkable, and he quickly fit into the team's style of fast-break offense, in which the well aimed pass is as important as the accurately directed shot.

"Right now," he said midway through his second season, "John Havlicek is the team's offensive leader. He runs the show, and he should, for he is as smart and as dedicated a player as I have ever seen. But I feel the coach is grooming me to take over the offense, and it will be a great responsibility. I have to work more on my defense and my ball-handling. But if I can't get this team to move, and if I can't get the ball to the men who have to do the scoring, then I won't be doing the job they expect me to do."

Heinsohn is as pleased with White as he is with Cowens.

"I feel that in order to have a great team, all five guys must be equally important. But if you have a good big-man and a good guard, you are at least halfway there. I think both Dave and Jo Jo are going to be great players, and because of that, the Celtics are going to be a great team."

The eight precocious stars discussed have come through their first seasons, their apprenticeships, with the gilt-edged credentials of winners, potential superstars. They have proved to the fans, the coaches, and the established stars that room will have to be made for them.

Their names are Lew Alcindor, Calvin Murphy, Pete Maravich, Neal Walk, Bob Lanier, Geoff Petrie, Dave Cowens, and Jo Jo White.

Their stories belong here. Their attempts to reach the top and their methods of achieving success are worthy of emulation and recognition. They have, indeed, emerged as winners in their personal battles. We have analyzed the making of eight basketball rookies, and each, in its unique way, is an inspirational success story.